MW01204261

The Big Book of Hypnotic Interventions

The Big Book of Hypnotic Interventions

A Desktop Companion for the Professional Hypnotherapist

Randy J. Hartman, M.A.

Writers Club Press
San Jose New York Lincoln Shanghai

The Big Book of Hypnotic Interventions
A Desktop Companion for the Professional Hypnotherapist

All Rights Reserved © 2000 by Randy J. Hartman

No part of this book may be reproduced or transmitted in any form
or by any means, graphic, electronic, or mechanical, including photocopying,
recording, taping, or by any information storage retrieval system,
without the permission in writing from the publisher.

Writers Club Press
an imprint of iUniverse.com, Inc.

For information address:
iUniverse.com, Inc.
620 North 48th Street, Suite 201
Lincoln, NE 68504-3467
www.iuniverse.com

ISBN: 0-595-14226-5

Printed in the United States of America

TABLE OF CONTENTS

INTRODUCTION

The Big Book of Hypnotic Interventions is designed to be a desktop reference for the professional hypnotherapist. The book is spiral bound for ease of use, and the scripts are double-spaced for ease of reading. What I have tried to provide here is a very wide variety of hypnotic oriented interventions. These interventions are at least a starting point with the problems the patients present with. I would encourage you to use these interventions as a framework, and then "tailor" the interventions to meet the needs of the individual patient.

Hypnotic interventions are no more than creativity in motion. No doubt, some of the best interventions are created and "off the cuff" during hypnotic sessions. If you can keep your creativity working you can expect to achieve some very wonderful successes. Some of the time the creativity can be sparked by reading case histories or a book such as this, or other times, just going with intuition, that gut level feeling. It is important to remember that not all the interventions will work all the time, for all of your patients.

Some of the real keys to being a successful hypnotherapist are continuing education in the field, the power of association with your professional peers, and your ability to be creative. At times it may seem risky to take the chance to be innovative, but without innovation we will not have any real forward movement in this profession. The possibilities with hypnosis seem boundless, new milestones are being documented frequently. I challenge you to move forward and set new milestones for others to follow.

We are on the threshold of an exciting and critical turning point in the history of therapeutic hypnosis. For over 200 years, since the generally recognized beginnings of hypnosis in the work of Anton Mesmer, hypnosis is starting to regain its respectability in the healing profession and with the general public. Let us all march proudly forward into the bright future that lies before us.

DISCOVERING ANXIETY

This script is a good direct approach to helping patients with general anxiety problems, borderline personalities should be excluded from this intervention.

Take the patient down into trance to a medium state and read the following script while pacing their breathing pattern.

We both know that you can scare yourself, because you have an active mind and a reactive body, and if you think that scary thing, even for a brief moment that it has been scaring you, but we also both know that there are other things you can think that are comfortable and calming, relaxing and reassuring thoughts or images that you can use instead to replace those other thoughts, to help you relax, to maintain that relaxed, calm feeling, you can let your unconscious mind learn all it needs to know to be able to distract you from those scary thoughts, to be able to provide you with those relaxing thoughts, and I think you will enjoy being happily unconcerned, unable to remember to worry in exactly the same way or at the same time, so from now on, when you enter that situation, you can enter it knowing you're protected and can tell that part of you that tries to do its job by telling you that there are things to be afraid of here, that you really don't need it any more, and don't want to hear it any more, and so it can either go away, or find a different game to play, and remind you instead of the good things that might happen here, or the fun things that might occur later, because those old thoughts and fears aren't useful anymore, so you can relax and forget it, and go on about your business surprised to discover that you have been thinking about something else entirely, and you will know at that point, deep down in every cell in your body, that you won't have to feel that again, that it is over and done with, even more rapidly than you expected, not as soon as you would have liked, you can do it, now, and you can do it later, you can frighten yourself with that thought, or you can calmly relax yourself with a different thought, that's right, so practice and choose, it all belongs to you.

(Continue intervention or go to trance termination)

Anxiety Script

It is recommended to use this metaphor for patients with panic attacks and general anxiety.

Take the patient to at least a medium state of trance and tell this story as you continue to pace their breathing.

It has been suggested, by a French physician, that when babies are born, they should not be held upside down, in a cold, bright, noisy operating room, and spanked to make them cry, instead they should be born into a warm, quiet room with soft, gentle lights and put into a warm bath, because when they are treated that way, they open their eyes and look around, they seem amazed and happy, they even seem to smile, they lie there quietly relaxed, and they grow up to be happier and more secure, all because they were treated gently, protected and taken care of, not hurt or scared, but just allowed to be safe and quiet for a while, a natural way of doing things that seems to work out well, because almost all animals have their babies on warm spring nights when it is safe to be born, and the mother can take care of them, and help them get used to things, slowly and comfortably adjust to things, and learn how to keep things under control, they learn to hide quietly in the tall grass, how to remain very still, even when there is danger near, and they learn to play happily, secure in the awareness that someone is nearby, protecting them, calmly watching out for them, and as they get older and wiser, they seem to calm down themselves, and become more quiet inside and out, as they use everything they've learned, because even a brief moment can provide a lesson to be used to keep oneself calm and quiet inside, the way warm water can seep throughout, even though only a small corner rests gently in that warm bath where a new born child rests and smiles, with a warm glow of safe comfort.

(Continue with intervention or go to trance termination)

FAST PHOBIA CURE (MODIFIED)

This procedure works usually in one session. It is most important to verify that the patient does have a phobia and the phobia interferes with trying to have a normal lifestyle. We must remember that fear is normal, even healthy at times. It is our internal warning system that we should listen to. The procedure is simple and normally only takes about thirty minutes.

1. Verify phobia, fight or flight?

2. Establish trance state and ideomotor signaling.

3. Establish a 3-place dissociation.
   a) Walk into the theater and look around.
   b) Have a seat in the middle of the theater.
   c) Float out of body, back to projection booth (look through window and stay in booth).

4. Run black & white movie.
   a) See still black & white picture of self prior to the phobic Response.
   b) Turn still black & white picture into a movie. Play through experience to point of safety afterwards and turn back into a still picture.

5. Run movie backwards.
   a) Leave booth, walk past self seated up to screen.
   b) Turn picture into color.
   c) Step into screen—experience.

d)   Play movie backwards "fast" 2 seconds or less through phobic experience to point of the first still picture and stop. Do this at least three times.

6.   Run the movie forward.
   a)   Movie at normal speed.
   b)   Observe client for phobic reaction.
   c)   If phobic reaction returns, repeat the process.

You can start this procedure without inducing trance. as the client turns his thoughts inwards, he will enter into a trance-like state. this procedure can also be done after the formal introduction of trance and ideomoter signaling is established.

RAISING SELF ESTEEM

This is a long-standing problem for many people in our society. Take the patient to at least a medium state of trance and read the following script while pacing the patient's breathing. Reinforce in future sessions as needed.

Do you know of Beethoven, who became increasingly deaf as he got older, but kept on working, writing music that he could not hear, until one day, one evening, he conducted the symphony as they played his newest work, a concerto, and when it was finished the crowd erupted in applause, they stood and cheered, but he could not hear, he stood there facing the orchestra, unaware of the audience's approval until someone walked out and turned him around so he could see what he could not hear, only then did he know what everyone needs to know, but sometimes can't hear, like the woman I have heard of, black hair, black eyes, stocky build, a bright professional woman who hated herself and hated her life, she thought she was ugly and awful, and she thought that was why so many awful things had happened to her, but one day she was having lunch with a friend, an artist she had known for a time, and she said to her friend, that there were so many beautiful women, and they all seemed to be on that street that day, and her friend simply said, I think you're the most beautiful woman I've ever seen, and went on eating, as if it were nothing, and that simple observation, that simply statement of opinion, matter of fact, not flattery, wouldn't go away, couldn't be undone, her friend was an artist who knew what beauty was, so she could not ignore it, and she could not forget it, instead she begin to look at herself, each day in the mirror, and she began to look at others, how they looked, who they were with, and it was very hard and scary at first to realize how wrong she had been, how wrong her mother had been, how wrong she had been about herself in so many different ways, but over time she had began to accept it, she was not ugly, she was not stupid, she was not a bad person, she was attractive and likeable and nice, and she did not have to settle for less than she deserved, how she thought changed, how she felt changed, what she did changed, her life changed, all because of one brief comment, one brief glimpse of herself, a clear admission of something she had been unable to let herself know before, that truth is beauty and beauty truth, and the truth about oneself, one's beauty, is in the eye of the beholder, but what we hear is not always measured on a hearing test, Beethoven heard things in his mind that his ears could no longer hear, and many animals can hear sounds, that the human ear cannot, and all we ever need to hear is that there is nothing else we need to do, except hear the beauty of what is.

(Terminate trance)

Six Step Reframe (Modified)

This NLP intervention is a good all around tool for dealing with habits. The procedure allows the patient to draw upon their own internal resources to reach an effective outcome to their presenting problem. With your patient arriving at their own decisions that fit their model of the world, they are more likely to find success.

Identify behavior to be changed.

Example: I want to stop smoking, but can't. I want to be a non-smoker, but something stops me.

Induce trance; take client to a working state.

Separate the conscious from the subconscious state.

Install ideomoter signaling; one for yes, two for no.

Ask the part to communicate with you; "Will the part of (name) subconscious that allows him to smoke, communicate with me?"

Notice response (yes/no)

Thank the part for communicating.

Verify that the part is the subconscious: "Is this the subconscious part that controls (name) smoking behavior?"

Once this second verification is complete, again, thank the part for communicating with you.

Ask the question; "Are you willing to let me know what your positive function/intention is?" Ask the client to state the positive intention.

Notice response, thank the part for communicating.

If there were ways to accomplish your positive function that would work as well as, or better than the present (behavior to be changed) would you be interested in trying them out?

If you get a no response, proceed with the refraining, presupposing a positive intention.

Access the creative part; "will the creative part of (name) communicate with me?" notice response.

Ask the creative part to generate at least three new and acceptable alternative behaviors that work as good, or better than the unwanted behavior. Ask the client to signal "yes" when each new behavior is arrived at.

Future pace: "Are you willing to take responsibility for using the three new alternatives in an appropriate context?" Notice response, if "no", or "no response", return to searching for new alternatives. Thank the creative part for its cooperation.

Ecology check: Are there any parts that object to the new alternatives? Notice response, if yes, return to the creative part for other alternatives. If parts still object, then negotiate between parts.

Closing frame: Thank all the parts for their cooperation and participation. ask the conscious mind to rejoin.

If the undesired behavior returns in the future, repeat the process as soon as possible.

ULCER SCRIPT

This is a good intervention for your patients that suffer from ulcers. The problem of ulcers is fairly common with middle and late stage alcoholics. Use this in trance when the client is deepened to a medium state, always pacing the breathing during trance.

Everyone is familiar with Smokey the Bear, and his pleas with campers to make sure their fires are completely out, so every scout learns how to put fires out, to make sure everything is cool, nothing left smoldering or hot, by pouring water on it, or dumping snow on it, just the way you're suppose to, keeping it cool while relaxing in the shade drinking a tall glass of ice water and watching that coolness spread, making sure it's completely out so you can leave the woods feeling relaxed and calm knowing nothing will catch and spread, because fire is to hot to handle unless you wear special gloves, insulated and made of fireproof materials which used to be very thick and heavy, but now there is a new material coated with a very thin layer of metal which is shiny and reflects all the heat, and keeps everything cool, even down to absolute zero, which is as cold as things can get, but they cool off nuclear reactors in a very different way, because when a reactor gets hot it means there are to many electrons flying around inside, so they lower in carbon rods that absorbs those electrons, absorbs all that energy, and as things quiet down, they also cool off, like turning off a spigot to quiet that dripping sound, shutting off the valve that stops the flow in there, they can also coat the walls with something cool and thick, like they do in houses, to insulate and protect, to keep the people inside comfortable in any weather, the way skin protects us from many things, but when it gets cut or scratched it needs to grow back together to heal that tiny hole, and so we take care of it, put a band-aide over it, and are careful not to bump it, not to irritate it, because it's okay to irritate things, to keep them cool and wet, but we try not to irritate things, especially not wild animals that live in forests and parks, the places we're suppose to protect by putting those fires out, the way rangers do, always looking out for smoke and rushing to put it out, before it gets out of control, which you can do too, wherever you go, wherever you are, even asleep at night, when those alarms begin to sound, putting it out without a thought, and returning to a deep, restful sleep, secure in this awareness, that you can take care of you. (Terminate trance)

THE JOURNEY OF LEARNING

This intervention allows the patient to look into their mind's eye to the future so they may decide for himself what behavioral changes they wish to address.

Picture yourself walking slowly down the mountain, becoming more relaxed with each step you take. Each breeze that caresses your body relaxes you more and more. The path is made up of switchbacks, and each time you change direction you'll double your relaxation (Pause). You're about a third of the way down the mountain, enjoying every step, feeling a comfortable breeze blowing, keeping you not too hot and not too cool, but just right. You stop and look up at the clouds against a beautiful blue sky. Take a deep breath now, and peacefulness overtakes you and you continue down, deeper down the mountain. You've become more relaxed with each step that is taken. allowing every muscle in your face, neck and shoulders to let go of any tension. Your legs and feet feel great; walking down the mountain brings pleasure to your heart and body (Pause). You are half way down the mountain You see a place to stop and take a break. There is a tree and a stream and you are able to watch the birds fly about, taking some time to relax yourself deeper, deeper relaxed than you've been before (Pause). Its now time to journey to the bottom of the mountain and relax much more deeply now, down, down slowly deeper down the mountain in complete joy, peace, strength and energy. Nothing bothers you; nothing disturbs you in any way. The peace that passes all understanding is yours. Feelings of love and acceptance of who you are are yours. As you reach the bottom of the mountain you notice a fork in the path. You must make a decision which path to take. If you go to the left, you will experience your future with no changes. If you choose to go to the right, you can experience the changes you want to make now. First let us experience the left path; keeping all your behaviors, beliefs, and attitudes, see what your life is like for you now. What is it costing you physically, emotionally, spiritually and financially? (Short pause) How do you feel? What do you say to yourself? (8-second pause) Now go 5 years into the future. Look at yourself in the mirror; are you happy with what you see? (Short pause)What are your behaviors costing you? Financially, emotionally, socially and spiritually? (5-second pause) How do you feel about yourself? (Pause) What are you saying to yourself while you look into the mirror? (Pause) Now lets go ten years into the future. Look at yourself in the mirror; are you happy with what you see? (Pause) What are your behaviors costing you? Financially, emotionally, socially and spiritually? (Pause) How do you feel about yourself? (Pause) What are you saying to yourself while you look into the mirror? (Pause) Now I want you to go to the time when you're rocking in a rocking chair and reflecting on your whole life, what do you say to yourself? (Pause) What do you wish you had done differently? (Pause) What behaviors do you wish you had changed? What attitudes have hindered you? What beliefs about you and others have limited you? Is this the life you wanted? what learning can aid you back in the present? (Pause) Come back now to the crossroads and let's travel the path to the right. Take a couple of nice deep breaths, letting go. Now in your mind's eye experience yourself making the changes that are important to you. (Pause) Who you are tomorrow depends on the decisions you make today. Behaviors you want to change, beliefs about yourself that are limiting you. What new beliefs could you now believe about yourself and others? (Pause) What new attitudes can enhance your life? (Pause) Now let's journey one year into your future, look in the mirror. See some of the positive changes that have taken place. How do you feel? (Pause) What do you say to yourself? (Pause) How have these changes affected you emotionally, socially, physically and financially? (Pause) What other areas in your life are different? (Pause) Now go five years into the future, look at yourself in the mirror, how happy are you with the changes you've made? (Pause) How have the changes affected you? (Pause) Look into that mirror, what do you say to yourself? (Pause) Now go ten years into the future, look at yourself in the mirror, how happy are you with the changes you've made? (Pause) How have the changes affected you? (Pause) Look into the mirror, what do you say to yourself? (Pause) Now go twenty years into the future, look at yourself in the mirror, how happy are you with the changes you've made? (Pause) How have the changes affected you? (Pause) Look into the mirror, what do you say to yourself? (Pause) Now go fifty years into the future, look at yourself in the mirror, how happy are you now with the changes you have made? (Pause) How have these changes affected you? (Pause) Look into the mirror again, what do you say to yourself? (Pause) Now I want you to go to the time when you are rocking in a rocking chair, reflecting on your whole life. See how making one or two changes can make a difference on the outcome of your life. A change in a behavior, belief or attitude can have a rippling effect in many ways and in many areas of your life. How is your life richer financially? (Pause) How is your life richer spiritually? (Pause) What have been the benefits in terms of significant others, family, friends and others? (Pause) What other areas of your life have you improved? (Pause) Now what are you saying to yourself? (Pause) How do you feel about yourself knowing changes have taken place? (Pause) What is it like to looking the mirror at yourself? Enjoy it, intensify it! Come back to the present, today, and know that all of it is yours, the choices are yours. (Terminate trance)

MEETING THE INNER CHILD

The purpose of this exercise is to assist the patient in getting in touch with his inner child. This in itself should generate insight for the patients as to what his present needs might be, and lend additional insight into life long behaviors.

Take client down in trance to a medium state.

Tell the patient the following story pacing his breathing throughout trance.

Think back now to when you were 7 or 8 years old (Pause), now picture in your mind the place you lived when you were that age (Pause). Now imagine that you are standing outside that very place looking at it, now walk around to the door you mainly used when you were a child, slowly now open the door and walk in, notice the sights, sounds and smells that were familiar to you (Pause). Continue to walk to the room where you used to feel the most secure and comfortable in. There as that 7 or 8 year old child, notice what you are doing, how were you dressed? (Pause) Now tell the child the most important/valuable information that he or she can use in his coming years now that you are an adult and have lived those years (Pause). Go ahead now and speak to the child and tell him what he needs to know (Pause). Now give the child a hug before you leave, if you can't hug the child, and then just say good-bye (Pause). Now turn and walk back out the same way you came in. Continue to walk to the location where you first viewed the place where you lived (Terminate trance ensuring that you empower the client's memory).

You can expect this experience to be very impactful and profound for some clients. You need to ask your clients to explain their experience in detail to you from start to finish. This experience should help build insight and possibly identify issues to be resolved in the future.

Migraine Headache Intervention Script

Initiate this script after taking the patient into a medium state of trance and continue to pace their breathing throughout the trance experience.

Now while you relax and allow yourself to experience the variety of changes that occur as you drift into a trance, I would like to help you to learn how to change those things that will allow you to be able to prevent or reduce your headaches, and the thing you need to learn is this, that when you feel a headache coming on, what you need to do is be able to allow your hands, and feet, to become very warm or hot very quickly, so as you pay attention to those hands and feet, I would like you to realize that you can imagine how it feels to have those hands and feet sitting in the hot rays of the sun…. or resting in the warm water of a bath…. or whatever other image comes to mind when you begin to pay attention to that warmth there…. and begin to feel the warmth grow, getting warmer and warmer, almost hot, comfortably swollen and warm, a warmth that may seem to spread into the arms and legs after a time, and as that warmth grows and becomes more clear in your awareness, you can continue to relax and drift down into a comfortable trance state, where your unconscious mind can find it's own way to let your mind become aware of that warmth and heaviness, a growing warmth and relaxation in the fingers of that hand, and the other hand, and the feet in your shoes, and your arms and legs too, perhaps, heavy and warm, warm and heavy, that's right, and from now on whenever you feel a headache coming on, what you need to do, and can do, is to relax in this way, remembering the quiet heaviness, and allow that warm thought to return, greater than before perhaps, until you feel that warmth everywhere, or just in those hands and feet, because now you can buy gloves and socks that heat up by themselves, powered by little batteries that make those thick gloves warm, and make those soft socks hot, almost as soon as you put them on, they begin to get warmer and warmer, you can try them on in a store and actually feel that heat increase, as they give off their own heat, a surprising feeling of warmth that works so well, they use them in alaska where even the bitter cold is soon replaced by the pulsating warmth, as those gloves heat up, and those socks heat up, and the hands and feet begin to thaw, begin to feel soft, swollen and warm, swollen with a comfortable feeling that spreads up the arms, and it continues on with you even after you drift upwards to a wakeful awareness, and reach that point where the eyes open, that's right, drifting upwards now, as that warm feeling continues, a nice warm feeling that you can create anytime you need to, anytime you want to, that's right, a warm wakefulness now, as the mind drifts up and the eyes are allowed to open. (Terminate trance)

BALLOON TECHNIQUE

This technique can be used for intervention with various problems: i.e. grieving, stop smoking and habit control.

During the assessment interview note the significant points that stops a person from achieving the desired change.

Take the patient into trance, deepen to somnambulism.

Ask the patient to go to his special place, a place that he feels comfortable, safe and secure. Build the intensity of his special place.

Sample script/example for stop smoking and the significant points to overcome are for; (1) Craving tobacco (2) Light headiness (3) Unspecified anxiety.

Enjoying your special place, knowing that you are comfortable and safe there, notice the colors about your special place, how very nice, notice all the other things about your special place, the sights, the sounds, the colors, no one else can be in your special place unless you allow them, what a wonderful place to be, so comfortable and safe in your special place, so wonderful, notice how you feel, comfortable and safe, enjoying your special place. Notice that in your (left) (right) hand you are holding three balloons, three of the ugliest balloons you have ever seen in your life, these ugly balloons look so out of place in your special place, these are such ugly repulsive colors on these balloons, the first balloon has the words, "craving tobacco" written on the side, the words are clear and easy to read, the second ugly balloon has the words "light headiness" clearly printed on the side, the third ugly balloon has the word "anxiety" clearly on the side, there you stand with these three very ugly balloons with the words, "craving tobacco", "light headiness" and "anxiety" written on the balloons, ugly balloons certainly do not belong in your special place, as you observe these ugly balloons with the words on them, you realize even more that they don't belong in your special, beautiful place, when you are ready you can release these ugly balloons and watch them slowly float up and away, moving slowly out of sight, as the balloons start to fade away, so do the words printed on them, remembering briefly that the words were "craving tobacco", "light headiness" and "anxiety", watch them slowly disappear from sight (Pause). Now you can see yourself in your special place, free of the ugly balloons, free of the tobacco craving, light headiness and anxiety, seeing yourself in your special place as a non smoker, noticing how you look now, how wonderful, notice how very wonderful you feel, feeling so proud of yourself now that you are a nonsmoker, how wonderful to be so rightfully proud of yourself, seeing yourself as a nonsmoker, experiencing how it feels to be a nonsmoker, how wonderful. Continue to relax, perhaps moving even one level deeper, enjoying the experience of being a nonsmoker. Bring client out of trance and process the experience.

GRIEVING A LOSS

This script is good for patients who have lost a significant someone or some part of themselves.

Take the patient to at least a medium state of trance and read the script while pacing their breathing pattern.

I wonder if you have ever seen the small fragile glass figurines that artisans sell at fairs and in shopping malls, made of tiny strands of clear bright glass all carefully laced together to form the shape of a ship or an animal, or even a house or a tree, that seemed to fascinate children with their delicate sparkles and shapes, like priceless jewels, valuable possessions, to be carried in velvet cases and protected, kept safe from loss or damage, tiny treasures, a gift to someone, like the treasure carried in ships across the sea, there was a program on TV several years ago, about a man who spent twenty years searching for such a ship, a lost treasure ship, one of hundreds that had been lost along the coast because of accidents and disasters and wars, he researched it very carefully, and though he knew exactly what had been lost, he also thought he knew what happened and where the treasure had sunk, but it was hard to find that ship, it had been lost for so long, it had gotten buried with mud and coral, and there were many other wrecks in the area, any one of which could have been the one, but wasn't, so he spent many years searching, and he raised thousands of dollars from investors, because he was convinced that there was something of great value down there, a lost treasure of immeasurable worth, and he convinced others it was there too, one day the divers returned to the surface shouting and screaming and holding up gold bars, they had found that ship, and it contained more than you could imagine, tons of gold bars, silver bars, gold coins, treasures untold, things from the past that had gone untouched, that had not been seen for hundreds of years suddenly were there for people to hold and to feel, and they held them with reverence, touching them gently and silently, as if these things that had been lost for so long, contained some memory of the past, something special that people need, something special to protect, like those tiny glass figures that you see at fairs and malls, they seem to be so fragile, so easily broken by someone rough, but they actually are quite sturdy and can survive for years and years, even when lost or hidden away, like the treasures at the bottom of the ocean, hidden deep down below, something precious and valuable inside, a part of you before, that belonged to you before, and the joy of its discovery, the recovery of that buried treasure, the pleasure of knowing it belongs to you, something you can bring back with you, that warm good part of the heart of the matter that children sometimes lose for a time, or have taken from them at another time, but it always lies there waiting to be brought back to the surface where it can be touched and protected and kept close to you forever, because it all belongs to you.

(Terminate trance)

HYPNOTIC ANTABUSE

This is a form of hypnotic aversion therapy that applies to all habits, alcohol, drug, tobacco, etc.

Possible uses
1. Adults who have been medically denied.
2. Adolescents, 13-19 years old.
3. There must be some expressed desire to abstain.

Do not use
1. If the patient has a "bleeding ulcer".
2. If a client refuses to consent.

To install
1. Post-hypnotic suggestion to the subconscious.
2. Describe the desired reaction in detail.
3. Reinforce 2-3 times during trance.
4. Follow-up at least once weekly and reinforce as needed.

Safety feature
The suggestion will be voided by the subconscious if the individual should start to approach a state of danger to themselves. Some patients, despite their good intentions will have to test this by using it so the safety feature becomes a safety valve in the event the patient's life is in danger.

SWISH PATTERN (NLP)

This procedure is multipurpose in nature. it can apply to drinking, smoking, nail biting, PTSD, and almost any habit. Start by verifying the trance state.

1. Ask the client to recall the undesired pictures/situation as if they were watching a movie screen. Install ideomoter signaling.
2. Have them run the picture on the movie screen up to the worst part (apex), and signal you when it occurs.
3. At this point, ask the client to "freeze" that picture on the screen.
4. Instruct the client to visualize a nice, wonderful image in one corner of the screen.
5. Then tell them that the nice scene is starting to grow, and slowly allow it to grow and over take the negative picture (Be patient and slowly talk them through it).
6. Ecology check: After trance ask the client to recall the negative picture and observe for any reactions. If a reaction is still present, then you may need to reinforce the technique.

ADULTS WITH ABUSE CHILDHOOD ISSUES

Application: For those patients still bothered by childhood abuse issues, physical, emotional and sexual.

Move the patient down in trance to a medium state, read the following script slowly as you continue to pace the-client's breathing throughout trance.

You know, and I know, that nothing can undo what happened to you in the past, what was to you was done to you back then, but that was then, and this is now, you can stop the pain and fear, you can put an end to it, now, and you already know how, you know how to forget to pay attention to particular things, you know how to shut doors and windows on the past, you know how to see things now for what they are now, not what was, and your unconscious knows how to walk forward in time across that line, a boundary line that marks a new beginning, that lets you join the present, as you let go of the past, that lets you see a future, when you will remember how good it felt today to let go of that past, to say goodbye to it, and to let yourself feel okay, so go ahead now and keep going ahead later on, because that past is through and you are just you here and now, and when you get home, there is something you can do to put this away and get on with the future, some way for you, a ritual perhaps, a ceremonial letting go, throwing something away to let yourself know that the past is done and the future has begun, and you will do that, will you not? (Terminate trance)

CONTROLLING RELATIONSHIPS

This script can be very helpful for those who feel they have to control the other person in their relationship, and have decided they want to give up their control.

Take the patient down in trance to a medium state and read the script while pacing their breathing pattern.

As you continue to relax, enjoying the beautiful feelings of trance, there is a story I know that I wanted to share with you, I'm sure in the story you will find much wisdom, the story is about a little boy and his turtle, the boy and his turtle were very close to each other and spent much of the summer days together, on the first day of school the little boy told his turtle that it had to stay in the house until he returned from school in the evening, and that evening when the little boy returned from school he discovered the turtle outside the house, the little boy scolded the turtle for disobeying, and told the turtle if he left the house without him that he would surely lose his friend, someone else would take the turtle for their friend, and then he would be alone. So the next day when the boy returned from school the turtle was outside the house again, once again the boy scolded the turtle, the next morning before the boy left for school he put the turtle in a tire in the back yard with food and water to protect the turtle, again, when he returned from school that evening he found that the turtle had gotten out of the tire and was in the front yard waiting for him, the little boy was getting upset because he couldn't seem to control the turtle, so he built a wooden box with tall sides to contain his turtle while he was away from home, the next morning the boy put the turtle in the wooden box and commanded him to remain there until he returned from school that evening, upon the boy's return to home that evening, he once again found that the turtle had gotten free and was in the front yard waiting for him, the little boy was so upset, he was certain if he didn't control the turtle he would lose his best friend, the next morning before leaving for school the little boy felt desperate and nearly out of ideas to control his friend the turtle, before leaving for school the boy drove a nail into the turtle's hard shell, and attached a long string to it that he tied to a tree in the backyard, he felt confident now that the turtle would not wander about while he was gone, that evening when the little boy returned from school, he found his poor turtle in the front yard, bleeding and dying from pulling loose from the nail, just laying there about to die, waiting for his friend to return.

(Terminate trance, reinforce as needed in future sessions)

IMMUNE SYSTEM RESPONSE

This script applies to those patients that need to increase their immune system responses to infections.

Take the patient down in trance to a medium state and read the following script while pacing their breathing pattern.

There is a tree in Africa that has a special relationship with a particular kind of ant. The ants spend their entire life living in that tree, they build their nests out of its leaves, they only drink the particular kind of sap that tree produces and secretes, or eats the tiny berries it grows, they never leave that tree, because that tree provides everything they need, and this type of ant is the only insect that does live in that tree, whenever any other insect begins to crawl upon it or lands on one of its leaves the ant sentries send out an alarm, and all the other ants come running, they attack those foreign bodies and either destroy them or drive them away, and in this way they protect their tree from any invaders that might attack it, or even destroy it, they save the tree, and the tree saves them, there are many other examples of the same thing throughout the world, where one tiny creature protects a large one from dangerous invaders, and in each and every case they always seem to have a way of paying very close attention to anything that could be harmful, so that they know immediately if some thing was wrong, and what is wrong and they pay close attention to it so they can do some thing about it, to eliminate or fix it, just the way people do when they notice a pain in a foot, and they pay close attention to that discomfort so they can tell what it is, and get rid of that stone in the shoe, as long as nothing gets in the way, and they continue to pay close attention to the way the body reacts and amplifies that reaction the way they amplify the sound of an engine, to hear what's wrong and let the body take care of itself with the same amazing grace that those ants take care of that tree, automatically and continuously, rushing to do those things needed to heal and protect.

(Continue intervention or terminate the trance, reinforce in future sessions)

CHILD BIRTHING

Excellent script for child-birthing. The patient needs prior hypnotic work to deepen and construct her "special place" before entering this phase. Take the patient down to somnambulism and read the script slowly while pacing her breathing.

Imagine your special place and feel a sense of peace and calm flow through you. you feel relaxed, your back feels relaxed, your stomach feels relaxed and your baby is calm and relaxed, and now let yourself drift and float into a comfortable state of relaxation, now bring to your mind the tremendous love you feel for your baby...pause...just think about how much you want your baby, and how much love you have to give your baby...pause...now just imagine directing that love to your baby, surrounding the womb with love, imagine this love to be a soothing pastel light that envelopes your baby...pause...now say quietly in your own mind and direct your statement to the baby, "I love you and I am anxious for your arrival"....Pause now say quietly in your mind, "you are wanted"...pause again, "you are wanted". Pause...now just imagine that your baby is smiling and that he or she has received your message. Continue to relax, relax your body, as you continue to relax, imagine the birth day arriving, (insert due date) when you feel the first hints of labor, it will be easy for you to apply the lessons in proper breathing and muscle control. You are calm and relaxed, breathing correctly; whenever you feel discomfort you take your thoughts far away to your special place, you breathe evenly, you know exactly what needs to be done. Whenever you feel discomfort, you know what needs to be done, exactly what needs to be done. Imagine giving birth, pushing when you need to, breathing properly and feeling comfortable, your mind is far away in your special place, you experience the birth process, you feel yourself push and breathe, and you feel comfortable, in charge, relaxed. You are comfortable, in control, relaxed. your delivery is successful in every way, and when the baby arrives it is healthy and strong...pause...now imagine yourself home with your baby, you are a natural mother, you know instinctively how to care for your child. You are enjoying motherhood; you accept the changes in your life with enthusiasm, you see difficulties as challenges, and are able to meet your needs as well as the family's needs. Just see yourself smiling, feeling good about yourself and your life, see yourself as the attractive, capable and loving woman that you are (Pause). See yourself smiling, feeling good about yourself and your life. Now just relax in your special place for another moment and soon you can begin to return to full consciousness, feeling relaxed and refreshed.

(Terminate trance or reinforce trance work)

SPECIFIC SURGICAL PROCEDURE

This intervention is good for surgery on a specific body part, i.e., foot, hand, or jaw. This procedure can be modified for a general surgical procedure. Start this script after you have deepened your patient to somnambulism.

Focus your attention on one of your hands, direct all your attention on that hand, and begin to imagine that hand becoming numb, recall a time your hand fell asleep and how wooden your hand felt. as you numb your hand, imagine a tingling begin in your fingertips and a warmth flow through your hand, soon all the feelings will drain out of your hand, all the feelings will drain away, and let this feeling be pleasant for you...now let that hand feel numb, completely numb. let all the feelings from your fingertips go, letting go of all the feeling from your fingertips to your wrist go, let it drain out of your hand, let it slowly drain out of your hand...let it drain out and imagine that hand feeling so numb...so numb...so very numb...you might begin to feel a warmth in the palm of that hand, a tingling in the fingertips, your hand feels heavy, and your hand feels as if it were made of wood, let all the feeling drain out, and let the hand be very numb...so very numb...very numb...as you concentrate on numbing that hand, you can feel yourself slipping safely, gently, deeper, deeper, deeper into a level of total relaxation. Just let that feeling go, and let that hand relax. You can feel it tingle, so numb...let it feel numb, wonderfully numb, let it fell so numb now. Let the feeling go, releasing it, let that hand feel so numb. It feels so very numb, as if it were wood. Your hand is now completely numb...notice the feeling, now place your numb hand on the part of the body (insert body part) that you want to numb, place your hand on your (insert body part) and now let the numbness drain out of your hand and into your (insert body part). Feel your (insert body part)

33

become numb, wooden like, heavy, numb, thick, as if it were made of wood. When all the numbness has left your hand, place your hand back down into a comfortable position. You can keep your (insert body part) numb for as long as you need to…when you have completed just let go and feel the numbness drain away, slowly draining away and your (insert body part) returns to normal, when you no longer need it to be numb, it returns to normal.

ACCESSING & REFRAMING MEMORIES OF SURGICAL ANESTHESIA

There are documented cases of patients remembering what was said during invasive surgical procedures while under general anesthesia. This will usually set up a posttraumatic stress disorder for the patient after surgery, or block their ability to submit to further surgery.

1. Trance induction and deepening with finger signaling:
   a. Initiate trance, set up ideomoter signaling with the patient.
   b. A deepening period of 30 minutes with relaxation, imagery, an so forth, with the following suggestion:
   "When your unconscious knows you are deep enough to shut out all sounds except my voice, your "yes" finger will lift".
   c. Age regress to time of surgery.

2. Physiological and ideodynamic accessing of meaningful sounds:
   a. "Does your unconscious mind recall having heard any disturbing sounds during the operation?"
   b. Step-by-step experience the entire operation utilizing ideomoter signaling.
   c. Therapeutic dissociation:
   "You can be a bystander just watching the whole thing. Your "yes" finger will lift if you hear anything disturbing to you".

3. Reframing and ratifying traumatic experience

a. "Please review the operation as it should have been conducted, with all the right things being said and done. As you are losing consciousness, your "yes" finger will lift; your "no" finger will lift each time something helpful is occurring; your "I don't want to answer" finger will lift as you are awakening".

b. *"Have* you learned anything from this review that would be helpful to you, and helpful for a surgeon to learn from you?"

c. "Will this more mature understanding of the situation now enable (whatever problem) to resolve itself in an entirely satisfactory way?"

Terminate trance and process the experience with the patient.

DIRECT HEALING SUGGESTIONS IN EMERGENCIES

All injured, frightened, hemorrhaging shocked, and unconscious people may be considered critically ill. They enter a hypnotic state spontaneously and need no formal trance induction.

1. Accessing healing sources
   a. Outline briefly and simply what is going to be done for them now.
   b. Designate a finger (by touching it lightly) to lift all by itself when the inner healing source (mind, brain, etc) carries out the following:
   c. "Your inner healing source can let this finger lift when the bleeding (and/or pain) has been turned down by half."
   d. "That finger can lift again when your comfort can continue getting better and better in every way."

2. Therapeutic facilitation
   a. "Your inner mind knows exactly what it needs to do to continue recovery by returning your blood pressure (or whatever) to normal. It can lift a finger to indicate that healing is continuing now all by itself."
   b. Congratulate the patient for being so relaxed and doing so well in allowing the healing to take place.
   c. Outline a series of steps (signs) by which the healing process will continue in the immediate future.

3. Ratification with posthypnotic suggestion

"You will feel yourself going into a deep, comfortable sleep for four hours and then waken feeling refreshed and alert with a good appetite" (Appropriate suggestions for each patient's particular situation are added at this point).

HEALING OF BURN INJURIES

The method will vary in relation to the surface extent and the depth of a burn. If a patient is seen hours or days after experiencing a burn, proceed as follows, explaining the process as a means of eliminating inflammation and allowing healing to occur rapidly. Install ideomotor signaling at the beginning of this procedure.

1. Accessing inner healing resources
"Remember a time when you walked into cold water. It felt cold for a while until a time when you got used to it. That represents a degree of numbness. When you are feeling cold at an unconscious level, your brain will shut down the messages that cause inflammation and interfere with healing. Imagine standing in cold water up to your knees. When you are feeling that unconsciously, your "yes" finger will lift. When you are half as sensitive as normal, your "no" finger will lift. Now, walk in further until the cold water is up to your hips. Your "yes" finger will lift when you are cold from your hips to your knees, and your "no" finger will lift when you are numb from your hips to your toes. Your right hand wrist will be below the water level and will also feel numb" (This will happen without explanation, even though the patient is lying in bed).

2. Self-testing of hypnotic analgesia
"Now you know how to make parts of your body alter sensations. Please place your cold, numb right hand over the burned area and experience the coldness and numbness flow into the burned area. When you

know the burn is cold and numb, your "yes" finger and "no" finger will lift to let me know how well you are doing."

3. Ratifying and maintaining healing
"That coldness and numbness will remain there for at least two hours. Then it may be necessary to repeat this exercise. You will get better each time you do it, and the result will last longer and work more effectively as you go along".

TRANSIENT (BRIEF) PAIN MANAGEMENT

Applications, Dental work, surgery, sports injuries, sprains, headaches, child-birthing.

Induce trance and read script pacing client's breathing pattern throughout the trance work.

You are sitting there comfortably aware that you have come here today because you want to gain control of your own abilities, to eliminate some future feelings of discomfort, and as you continue to relax and to drift down into a deep trance, I want you to take your time, not too fast, not too slow, because there are some things you need to listen to carefully, first you need to understand that you already have the ability to lose an arm or a hand, to become completely unaware of exactly where that arm is positioned, or what it is doing, and you have the ability to be not concerned about exactly where that arm is, or that hand or leg, or your entire body for that fact, this may seem to take too much effort to pay attention to at times, because you also have an unconscious ability you can learn how to use effectively, and that ability is to turn off the feeling in an arm, a leg, or anywhere you chose, and once you discover how it feels to not feel anything at all, wherever you want that to occur, then you can create the numb, comfortable feeling, anywhere, anytime it is useful to you, and I don't know whether your unconscious mind will allow you to discover that numb feeling in the right hand, or a finger of the left hand first, a tiny area of numbness, a comfortable tingling feeling, a heavy thick numbness, that seems to grow and spreads over time, until it covers that hand, the back of the hand, or anything else you pay close attention to, it's your choice, it just seems to disappear from your experience, but you don't know how it feels, to not feel something that isn't there, so here is what I

41

want you to do, I want you to reach over to that numb area, to that numb hand, that's right, go ahead and touch it, (pause), and feel that touching as you begin to pinch yourself there, at first you may experience a feeling, but as you continue to pinch yourself, an interesting thing happens (Slight pause), you begin to discover that there are times when you feel nothing at all there, that's right, the feeling just seems to disappear, as you continue to learn how to allow your unconscious mind to turn off those feelings, all you need to do is just pay very close attention to the numbness, and as that ability grows and develops, and you begin to know, really know beyond a doubt, that you already do know how to allow feeling and pain to disappear from your hand, or anywhere, your other hand can return to a resting place of its choice, and you can drift up to that point where wakeful awareness will return, so go ahead now, as you relax, and discover how to let go and to feel that numbness more and more clearly, and you can drift up more, in your own time, in your own comfortable way, that's right, take your time to learn, and then drifting back upwards, eyes opening (pause) now, before you wake up completely, I would like you to close your eyes again, and allow that drifting down again, reentering that place of calm relaxation, perhaps going even deeper than before, while you drift down again, there is a story I want to tell you about a young boy on TV not long ago in the past, he had learned to control all of his pain, he described the steps he went down in his mind, one at a time down those steps, until he found this hall at the bottom, like a long tunnel, and all along the tunnel on both sides were many different switches, switchboxes, each clearly labeled, one for the right hand, one for the left, one for the leg, and one for every place on the body, and he could see the wires to those switches clearly, the nerves that carried the feelings from one place to another, all going through those switches and switchboxes, all he needed to do was to reach up in his mind and turn off the switches he wanted to, and then he could feel nothing at all, no feelings could get through from there, no feelings at all, because he had turned off those switches, he used his mind's abilities differently from the man who simply made his body numb, he didn't know how he did it exactly, all he knew was he relaxed and disconnected, like a train car disconnecting from the rest, moved his mind away from his body, moving it outside some place else, where he could watch and listen, but drift off someplace else, and it really doesn't matter exactly how you tell your unconscious what to do, or how your unconscious does it for you, the only thing of importance is that you know you can lose the feelings as easily as closing your eyes, and drifting down within, where something unknown in the unconscious happens that allows you to disconnect from the uncomfortable feeling, that allows that numbness to occur.... and then a drifting upwards now, upwards towards the surface and slowly allowing the eyes to open as wakeful awareness returns with a comfortable continuation of that protected feeling of safe, secure relaxation and an ability to forget an arm, or anything at all, with no need to pay attention to things that are just fine, that somebody else can take care of while you drift in your mind, remaining secure in this new knowledge you have gained (Pause), now it is time to enjoy that comfortable drifting upwards where the eyes open, and wakeful awareness returns quite completely now. (Terminate trance)

If possible, before the client leaves your office, ask the client to practice making a body part numb. Ask the client to practice this as much as reasonably possible before the next session. Future sessions may or may not require repeating this session.

CHRONIC PAIN MANAGEMENT

Applications: Long term pain, back injuries, nerve damage, phantom limb pain, cancer.

Induce trance, read script pacing the patient's breathing pattern.

With your eyes closed, as you begin to relax, you probably see that the first thing you notice is how difficult it is to not become aware of that pain and discomfort, and that's fine, you don't need to fight your mind which is always aware of those sensations there for you, because as you relax, you can begin to discover that each time you relax a muscle in your arm...or a leg...or your face...or even a foot...or a finger, that you can drift down more and more deeply than before, into that sensation there in a more relaxed and comfortable way, because there really is no need to make the effort it takes to try to stay away from that feeling or to try to fight that feeling, which almost seems to guide and direct awareness down toward it, more and more into it, and as you drift toward it, toward that center of that feeling, everything else can be allowed to relax, to relax more and more, as you begin to discover that it really is okay to let go in that way, to allow yourself to relax every other part of your body and to drift down toward the very tiniest center of that feeling, the very small middle of it, the source of it, and then to drift down through that center into a place beneath it of quietness and calm awareness, down through that feeling, and out the other side, into a space of relaxed letting go, of comfortable relaxation, where the mind can drift, the way waves drift from one place to another as that body relaxes and the mind becomes smoother and smoother, able to absorb events, even those events, easily and comfortably, to become absorbed in thoughts and images, as the mind reflects the clear wonder of a child, a young child, watching a flock

44

of geese as they soar across the sky and fly into the mist, the rhythm of their sound becoming softer and softer, as soft as the down in a pillow in a place where you rest and relax, a most comfortable place for a child to relax and drift into dreams through the mind, protected and safe, where the letting go allows the flow and the soft floating upwards, where the mind drifts free of things far below, and seems to soar in a sky as clear as glass, so smooth and clear that it disappears when you look into it, and what appears instead is the deep blue shine of the warm soft sun, a star far beyond that reaches out and provides that warm soft light as you drift down and experience the comfort and learn to feel the sound sleep that your unconscious mind can provide you whenever you relax and allow it to drift into a trance, because it can take you down through that feeling, into a space, that relaxed comfortable place, as you relax and allow it to do so just for you, that relief and relaxation, that drifting down through which comes to you whenever you allow it to, just as that drifting upwards occurs as well, a drifting back toward the surface of wakeful awareness, as your unconscious mind reminds you to drift up in a relaxed, comfortable way, back towards the surface now, bring with you that comfortable relaxation, that automatic change in sensation, even as the mind drifts upwards, the relaxation continues, as the mind awakens and the eyes open, but the body remains behind, relaxed, that's right, eyes open now (pause) but before you come back completely, you can close those eyes again, and feel that relaxation again, and recognize that ability, that ability to relax, to let your unconscious mind find the way to provide you with more and more comfort, more and more relaxed, letting go, that's right, aware that you can do so, anytime, anyplace you need or want to, you can return to that place, so here is what you do, later on today, tomorrow, next week, and for the rest of your life, whenever you need to or want to, you can close your eyes just for a moment, perhaps, and feel that comfortable feeling, that change in sensation return to you, and you drift into that light trance, or a deep trance, where your unconscious mind can take care of you, make things comfortable for you, and then you return to the surface of wakeful awareness, not needing to make the effort it takes to try to tell if that feeling is there or not, just as you return now back to the surface, comfortably relaxed and refreshed, remaining relaxed perhaps.

HYPNOTIC APPROACHES IN PAIN MANAGEMENT

Amnesia: Help the patient forget about the pain via distraction.
a.   Do not use the word "pain".
b.   Do not remind the patient of the problem.
c.   Explain to the patient how the disassociation works.

Anesthesia: To remove or make numb the pain in a given area.
a.   Best not to remove 100% of the feelings. A patient may re-injure himself.
     Need to keep some feelings or the patient will feel somewhat handicapped.

Analgesia: Similar to anesthesia, but pain is removed/reduced, but the tactile sensation and pressure is still there.
a.   Use terms of analogies to remove pain.
b.   "Melting slowly away like a small ice cube".

Symptom Substitution: Replace original feelings with a better feeling.
a.   Describing pain as warm instead of cold.
b.   Describe pain as comfortably cool instead of hot.
c.   Working in direct opposition to the current feeling.

Teaching Disassociation: Teach the patient to disassociate from pain.
a.   "Leave the pain here and move to the other side of the room".
b.   "Taking your mind on a shopping trip to the mall".

c.   Confuse the patient, move the pain to a healthy area of the body so the pain can be dealt with efficiently.

Fractional Approach to Pain Management: Talking about the patient losing a percentage of pain.

a.   Start at 5%, then slowly move ahead in increments of 5% going to 90% of pain removal. then telling the patient we should settle for 80% of pain removed.

Autohypnosis: Putting the patient in charge of his pain management.

a.   Teach the patient how to go into trance by himself.
b.   Assist the patient in developing his suggestions using the rules of self-hypnosis.

Headache Relief Without Trance:
Having the patient visually disassociate from the headache.

a.   Have the patient assign a "color" to their headache.
b.   Ask them to turn that color a shade lighter.
c.   Continue going lighter, switching to other lighter colors as you go.
d.   Continue this procedure for 3 to 5 minutes.

Extra Thoughts...

If the patient still appears reluctant or doubtful, start with establishing a "yes" set to elicit a positive framework. Always be prepared to shift from one procedure to another if needed, it is very difficult to know in advance what will work best in that patient's model of the world.

IMPROVING STUDY HABITS

This intervention is especially good for high school and college students that feel the need to improve their study habits. Start this procedure at somnambulism.

You are going to experience a completely successful study period, a completely successful study period, you will (for example) study at a table near the window on the third floor of the library...now just imagine yourself comfortable as you prepare to study...you arrange your materials, your papers, your books in front of you, you take a deep breath. Exhale...and relax, take another deep breath, pause, exhale and relax, and you begin to focus on the work in front of you. You will begin at (insert time) and you will stop at (insert time). Within this block of time, you will focus completely on the work at hand because you are enthusiastic and eager to absorb all the information that you need. You concentrate completely, all the normal sounds around you fade out as you find yourself absorbed in your studies. You feel calm, relaxed, and nothing disturbs your concentration, and you work at your peak, absorbing and retaining all the information you need. When the time is up, a signal from your subconscious will alert you, tell you that you have completed your work, and you take a deep breath and you are relaxed and have plenty of energy for other activities.

Repeat this procedure as needed. Three times would be recommended for maximum effectiveness.

Stress Reduction Intervention

No doubt you will have numerous patients that this intervention will apply to as stress is a high profile problem in our society. Start this script when you have deepened the patient to the medium state.

Because you are now relaxed, let any feelings you have buried come up to the surface, examine those feelings, decide which ones you want to keep and which ones you want to discard...keep the ones you need right now, and cast away the others. It is all right for you to feel sad or depressed sometimes. It is your way of being good to yourself. Depression is a healing process so you can allow yourself to mourn or be sad and when you have completed the time of sadness, set yourself free. You are good to yourself and the time will soon be over for those feelings and you will feel free from them. You will feel free because you can accept or discard any feelings you are through with. They are yours, and you can let them come and go, come and go as you need them. Now relax, and continue to relax, and feel yourself relaxed with your feelings, and think of how you are a whole person with many feelings that make you whole and healthy, and if any unwanted outside pressure comes at you, you are surrounded by a shield that protects you from pressure. The shield will protect you from pressure. The shield prevents outside pressure from invading you. Pressure bounces off and away from you, bounces off and away. No matter where it comes from, or who sends it, it just bounces off and away. It bounces off and away. You feel fine because the shield protects you all day from stress and pressure. You go through your day feeling fine. You watch the stress bounce off and away. The more stress outside, the calmer you feel inside. The calmer you feel inside. Calm inside. You are a calm person and you are shielded from stress. You act in ways that make you feel good. You now have new responses to old situations. This new response will make you feel strong and calm and free. Your days will be full of accomplishments, and you will be pleased with those accomplishments. You will feel good about yourself because you have new responses that are making your day more pleasant, you are calm and strong and free from stress. You are completely free from stress. You are free of all stress.

SLEEP ENHANCEMENT

This intervention should be adequate for patients that present with problems sleeping. Start this intervention at the medium state as you continue to pace the patient's breathing pattern.

Now just linger in your special place, there is no place to go, nothing to do. Just rest, just let yourself drift and float, drift and float into a sound and restful sleep, and as you drift deeper and deeper, visualize yourself lying in bed at night sleeping, notice how comfortable and relaxed you look...sleeping so soundly...appearing very comfortable, with no real effort when you go to bed every night, and as you lay there, I want you to think of nothing but the color blue...just let your thoughts fill with blue and make sure you try to do this every night before you finally let go. I know it will be difficult to experience nothing but the color blue, but I know you can do it for a while. So when my words come back to you, at night as you drift off to sleep you will remember to try to stay awake, at least for a little while to be aware of only the color blue. Like the blue in the sky...or a robin's egg blue...or the deep blue sea.

IMPROVED ATHLETIC PERFORMANCE

This intervention is geared to assist the athlete in improving their performance in their chosen sport.

Start the intervention in the medium state and continue pacing the patient's breathing pattern.

Imagine preparing yourself for the challenge, your equipment is good and is adjusted to your needs, you are prepared both physically and mentally, now just imagine for a moment stressful situations that may arise...such as the weather, the actions of another player, or field conditions, and see yourself react to these conditions in a cool, undisturbed way. Now review in your mind your entire game (or sport) from start to finish, see it in slow motion...see it in as much detail as you can. Review all the strategy you used...this perfect game, your perfect game, can be played again and again, imagine yourself reaching your goal, you have reached your goal. You have reached this goal and you can go on to other goals whenever you like. Now just imagine how you felt during your perfect game, imagine that confidence and ease, you were focused and strong; imagine yourself begin again, take a few deep breaths and in slow motion see every action, feel every move in the most positive way. See yourself act and react, move perfectly, every muscle in harmony with your thought, see your strategy, see yourself moving perfectly, see every perfect move, and now notice how you feel, you feel relaxed, at ease, strong, alert, and clear-minded, your vision is sharp, your reflects are perfect, you feel great, now see yourself conclude and win the challenge, you feel pleased with yourself, and every correct move, every play is imprinted into your subconscious so that you can repeat your perfect game over and over like a film, now go back and once again replay the sequence in your mind, and this time at normal speed, imagine the sequence from start to finish…and see it in great detail, in the greatest of detail, imagine making all the right moves and playing a terrific game, the best game you ever played.

Depending on the sport, you will need to tailor the language to meet the needs of the patient. Reinforcement is good, using a cassette tape with this intervention is ideal.

Self-Acceptance Intervention

This script is good for patients to learn and accept their own uniqueness as an individual.

Take the patient down in trance to a medium state and begin reading the script as you continue pacing their breathing.

As you have already guessed, there is no perfect way to relax or to enter into trance, because it happens naturally, it is always different each time, no two snowflakes are exactly alike, and even the fingerprints of twins differ, so who's to say which one is the right one, and which one is the left, and so no matter how hard we try to do things perfectly, the odd thing is we always prefer the thing that is different and unique, something that is one of a kind, like stamps printed upside down, or coins made a little bit wrong, those become prized collector's items, just because they are different from all the rest, even if you need a magnifying lens to see the imperfection, because we want to see things differently, to see things bigger or smaller than we think they are, like a mirror in a circus that changes our shape and form, so we can really see what different would be if different we really were, which may explain the collections in art museums around the world, on one wall is a Van Gogh, on another is a Picasso, their beauty and power stands out, but everything is out of place or out of proportion, two legs different lengths or two arms different sizes, and yet it is all art of the highest form, the different paintings, different styles, like clothing styles that change from one age to another, and yet each is beautiful and flattering in its own way, in the eye of the beholder every flower is unique, designed the way it should be to be exactly what it is, and that is why we used to play a game of sorts as children, to decide which flower we would be and which we already were, and then to really look at it later and be

56

surprised by what we found, something you can do as well, whenever you decide which flower you belong to, but for right now we don't need to know how you will feel when you decide to know that what seems wrong can be quite right after all, after you do all your homework and explore your own museum in the gardens of your mind where you can collect what you need to know to protect your own treasure and to treasure what you have collected even after you think you know that you really do not know what they really think about what you think about you.

(Continue with intervention or terminate trance)

PSYCHO PHYSIOLOGICAL INTERVENTION

This is a short and direct approach for helping patients with diagnoses of psycho physiological disorders.

Take the patient down into trance to a medium state and read this script while pacing their breathing.

As you relax in a deep trance now, deep enough, I would like to give your unconscious mind time to examine this problem of yours carefully, until it can find a beneficial solution, a solution you can use, a solution it is willing and able to use, to use for you to solve this problem, and to solve it comfortably and well, and when it knows that it can and will do so, has decided what to do, and has decided to do it for you, it can indicate that knowing, that decision, by creating a movement in a hand or a finger, or an arm maybe moved, or even a leg or a foot, just small movement so that you and I can know, so that it can indicate that it knows what to do, and is going to do it, so let's go ahead and just wait patiently, waiting for that unconscious signal, keep waiting until you know, until it lets you know somehow, that it knows how now, and will do it for you. (Pause until you detect movement, then go to trance termination)

MULTIPLE PERSONALITY MERGING SCRIPT

This script/metaphor is for use with patients with multiple personality disorders. It is important to bear in mind that this is only a small segment of treatment for mpd's.

Take the patient's base line personality in to trance to a medium state and pace their breathing as you tell them the following story.

While you drift, the mind drifts, like water from one place to another, automatically, effortlessly flowing, going the easiest way down toward the sea, and when you fly above it, you see the paths it takes, the tiny creeks and streams, that wind their way down the hills, down to the valleys below where they flow into the river, and that river flows along, getting larger and larger, gaining more and more from each new stream that joins it, and those rivers flow together, a larger river forms, and it flows too, it flows gently but surely towards the sea, it winds its way around mountains, it surges through the plains, gathering more and more strength, from other streams and rivers along the way, and eventually it reaches the bay, where it spreads throughout the delta and joins the power of the ocean, and becomes a part of that sea of life, a part of everything, and while you continue to relax, I would like to talk to all of you, to all the you's there are, because a bunch of yous' together can be a marvelous forest, and one you alone is just a tree in the middle of no where, when things join together they gain strength and protection from each other, it is a sign of the times, headlines in the newspaper each day describe the way small companies are forming large healthy companies by joining together, a merger of resources, several small banks announced a merger the other day and it was difficult to work out who would be in charge, but eventually they worked it out so that everyone was happy, everyone was represented, and each group had its say so that in a short time, when they change all their signs, and they change all the labels, no one will ever know that things weren't always that way, it will just seem to be the way its suppose to be to be together as one, to be one, like a special color that is several colors blended together to be a new color, a special color all its own in that painting a portrait perhaps of a family, a group of people living as one, where each has special abilities, and each has a special purpose to serve, but sometimes they begin to keep secrets from each other and the world, and when that happens they are brought together and told to tell each other those secrets they all need to know, because when mother has a secret, or father has a secret, or brother or sister have secrets, and they all have secrets from outsiders, the family begins to fall apart, and each member loses something, because they all need each other, and they all need to be loved by each other, but secrets keep them from each other, and they begin to be mean to each other, when they need to tell each other they are very, very sorry and they need to come together, to cry together, to love together, to share their lives and strengths so that when they have their portrait painted, they look like they belong together as one, and the artist can merge the colors as the relief and relaxation of them all, allow the minds to drift together, winding gently but surely toward the sea, where each can see and feel that secure feeling of belonging, here and now, safe and sound, because things change as relaxation occurs, and an openness provides a well deserved rest after the effort it took to overcome those problems and to join together as one.

Improved Memory Intervention

This intervention is especially good for students who complain of poor memory retention. Start this intervention at the medium state while continuing to pace the patient's breathing pattern.

Imagine yourself enjoying a day in your special place, imagine yourself relaxing, smiling, playing, and feeling comfortable, feeling so comfortable, imagine for a moment that all your cares are far away, imagine yourself lying down and stretching out. For the moment nothing is of any importance, nothing is of any consequence, you have given yourself some off and enjoy relaxing. As you watch the day drift bye, you feel so lazy, so relaxed, you notice a large piece of white paper drifting in the breeze, and soon the paper floats your way, and as it drops near you, you can read it and it has all the information that you need, all the information that you have learned. You now remember all that you have learned, remembering all that you have learned, you will remember it all. the information you learn will be clearly typed across a piece of white paper, and whenever you need to recall this information, you will imagine that paper and know exactly what is written on it. From now on whenever you need the information you have studied, all the information you need will be written on that large white paper.

WEIGHT MANAGEMENT

This weight management intervention can apply to all your patients that do not have a medical problem diagnosed as a part of the weight problem. Start this intervention once your patient is at somnambulism. Expect to reinforce this intervention in future sessions.

Because you are now at peace and relaxed, you can be successful at reaching any goal, at losing weight…you can imagine that you have lost the amount of weight you no longer want or need, and you have maintained that weight loss…you imagine and feel and think of yourself as slimmer, thinner, muscles tight, total body in shape. Your unconscious will now act on this image, and realize, and actualize this image. You will allow yourself to lose weight, lose the amount of weight you no longer want or need, and to maintain that weight loss. You change negative eating patterns into good eating patterns now…you allow this to take place easily and effortlessly, and now you imagine for a moment a table, a table in front of you, and you fill this table with foods that are harmful to you, foods that are harmful to your body and emotions…you imagine these foods; they are sweets, snack foods and junk foods, you place them on the table…these foods are all harmful to you, they are like poison in your system…these kinds of foods cause you to gain weight you no longer want or need. If you choose to eat any of these foods, you eat a small amount, a very small amount of these foods satisfies you completely. You couldn't eat another bite.…so now you push these foods off the table, push them away from you…your body rejects these foods. Your mind and emotions reject these foods, you clear the table, now on that empty table, you place the many foods that you enjoy anyway. Good healthful foods, foods that contain fewer calories, there are the fruits that you enjoy: Cool, clean and crisp. there are the vegetables that you enjoy, you see those good healthful foods on the table, and you imagine those good foods, and you eat slowly, very slowly, and you eat modest portions and then stop, and that feels fine. You eat correct and reasonable amounts, and you are totally satisfied, you are satisfied from one meal to the next, and have no desire to snack between meals. You feel totally proud of yourself, you reflect on all the positive things in your life, the goals and successes you have already achieved, and you know that you will continue to be successful, reaching every goal that you have, and creating the most healthy and positive life for yourself, and now you imagine seeing yourself, stomach flat, hips and thighs firm and slim...you look great and feel so good. You are relaxed and peaceful, and food is less and less important, and you are more comfortable eating slowly...snacking is unimportant to you, regardless of where you are, or what you are working on, at home or at work...you can eat small amounts of food in a restaurant, and you will eat more slowly...you may leave part of your meal on your plate, and that is fine...regardless of stress, you are more at peace and relaxed, and food is less important to you. You feel proud of yourself, the rewards are tremendous, and now whenever you think of eating, you choose those good healthful foods, and you eat the correct amount. When you have eaten the correct amount you stop eating, you can stop eating. You may even leave some food on your plate, and that is alright. You simply stop eating, and continue to relax and allow that sense of confidence and peace to now flow through you. You are more motivated now than ever before to create the most healthy and positive life for yourself, to change old eating patterns into good eating patterns, to lose the amount of weight you no longer want or need, and to maintain this weight loss. You now have new ways of dealing with your old habits, these new habits will make permanent weight loss possible. You feel wonderful, and you can begin to experience a new and healthy vital energy that flows through your body and mind, and your thoughts are positive, confident...you reflect on all the positive aspects about yourself, your intelligence and creativity, and you see yourself as the attractive person that you are, and you allow these positive feelings to grow stronger and stronger for you every day, every night, and now you continue to relax.

(Terminate trance or continue)

JEALOUSY INTERVENTION

This script is a short and direct approach for helping patients deal with their feelings of jealousy.

Take the patient down in trance to a medium state and read the script while pacing their breathing pattern.

Now you say that you recognize that you're to jealous, and I know what you need to do, if you really want to avoid that problem, but you won't want to do it, unless you really believe that (he) (she) merits your trust, and so the first thing to do is this: Decide now, here and now, once and for all, does this person deserve you, and deserve your love, or not? If they do, then they are trustworthy, if they don't, then you'd better get out, right now, as soon as you can, but if they are trustworthy enough to deserve you and your devotion, then here is what you need to do, because your jealousy is the meanest, the most obnoxious thing you can do to someone who cares about you, you need to apologize to that person, in every way you can, you need to get down on your knees, and tell them how sorry you are, for being so mean and cruel, for even thinking they could betray you, for not accepting their gift to you, because if you don't love them, then let go of them, and if you do love them, then you'd better say your sorry, and be adult enough to let them be an adult too, because if you keep acting like a mean, suspicious parent, its quite apparent to me, that you're using your imagination in a very unpleasant way, in ways that are quite painful to those you say you love, so the first step is to apologize for being so mean and cruel, for using your imagination in such a childish way, without any control at all, and you certainly should apologize for soiling this sacred ground, and creating a foul odor in the atmosphere of love, because you will feel so embarrassed if you do it again, that your face will flush, and you will blush, and that will be the last time you try to control what doesn't belong to you, but is a gift, a loan, that will be repossessed if you don't treat it right, so decide now what you're going to do, and what you're not going to do, and see if you have enough to do it, no matter what (Pause 8 seconds).

FEAR OF FAILURE INTERVENTION

This script is useful for patients with fear of failure and test anxiety.

Take the patient down in trance to a medium state and read this script while pacing their breathing.

Because everyone needs to relax at times, even Olympic athletes who are under great pressure to perform, and sometimes must be perfect to win, needs some way to relax, and to put things into perspective, to recognize that it is just a sport and not a war between nations, because a war is one thing and a game is something else entirely, especially in this atomic age where a war could mean the end of everything, we really cannot afford to make even the smallest of mistakes, and so some people are terrified that the failsafe system will fail, and that will be the end of it all, all because of some tiny little error, somebody doing something wrong or saying the wrong thing at the wrong time in the wrong way to the wrong person, and everything goes up in flames, which is why they have special programs, for the people working with those systems, because what they have to do is so dangerous and so terribly important that special training and counseling is required, the only place in the world, perhaps, where mistakes can not be allowed, and it is comforting to note that almost everyplace else, an error is just an opportunity to do it differently later on, because perfection is rarely required and perfection is seldom needed and even the Olympic athletes are never perfect all the time, and sometimes do things wrong like the Navahos when they weave a rug, who always leave a knot, an imperfection, so the gods won't be angered, and think they are trying to be gods themselves, but that is another story, about what is really important, and what is not, and how it feels to give permission to enjoy the feelings of the freedom to feel safe doing these things, knowing that the world won't end, if you leave a knot some place, so the gods can relax, knowing you are not challenging them, just doing the best you can, letting it go at that.

(Continue with intervention or terminate trance, reinforce as indicated)

AGE PROGRESSION

This procedure has also been dubbed "success therapy". by taking the patient to the future he can see himself doing all the right things at the correct time in the proper sequence. Basically it is rehearsal of a behavior in the future. This establishes an association of the familiarity of a desired response within a specific context.

1. Induction

2. Build a response set
    a. Use "future tense" in the hypnotic patter to move your client's mind into the future mode.

3. Metaphor/analogies regarding the future
    a. Design/use a metaphor or analogies to talk about positive future changes.

4. Identifying positive resources
    a. With your hypnotic patter, reinforce the client's ability to learn, adapt, and change.

5. Identify specific future contexts: Verbally review the specific situation(s)in a future context.
    a. Standard resource models are; learning, opportunities, loving, caring, adapting.
    b. Verbally "mark" (embedding) these positive words.

6. Rehearse behavioral sequence
   a. Incorporate those positive words while having the client see himself doing the task easily and competently in specific situations.
   b. Allow the client to have the subjective experience of having weeks and months of rehearsal within a single session by distorting time.

7. Generalization of resources
   a. Ask the client to see himself in other specific situations, not related to step seven.
   b. Allow about one minute of silence for the client to complete the task.

8. Posthypnotic suggestion
   a. Form a single, simple, non-complex suggestion that the client can take this new understanding with them into his life.

9. Terminate trance and debrief client.

AGE REGRESSION

Revivification:

The client withdraws into themselves and tries to recreate the world of their past; the personality of the regressed client will be changed and they will think and behave as they did at that point in time.

The first attempt at age regression should be to a point in the past that was a very positive, happy time for the client. The hypnotist can become a stranger to the client, making conversation and rapport more difficult. The problem is solved by transforming the hypnotist into someone known to the client during the earlier period.

Age Regression:

The client looks into the past only as an observer of events. A deep state of trance is necessary to produce age regression/revivification (Somnambulism).

It is recommended that you take the individual back in time in increments of five years using age, not dates, i.e. age 30 to age 25, etc. As the patient goes back through time it is important to remind them to only observe things and events in passing, or the patient may stop to engage a memory before getting to the target age. Some patients will have the ability to go into trance and without prompting return to the past event that needs to be dealt with. while other patients will need to be guided back through their life to the target age.

Blended Technique for Stop Smoking

Before putting the patient in trance, start with the following script and follow through. ensure that the patient's answers are stated in the positive. Do not accept an answer of "I don't know".

> What is your motivation to stop smoking?
> Why do you want to stop?
> Is it for yourself or someone else?
> When did you start smoking?
> What family members smoke?
> What is the qual4ty of the relationship with those people?
> What is most stressful to you?
> What is fun for you?
> What situations in the past prompted you to smoke?
> Where are you when you smoke?
> What are you doing when you smoke?
> What one word signifies to you complete relaxation?

"I want you to now think of that word in your mind and touch your thumb and your index finger together. From now on, each time you want to completely relax and use self-hypnosis, go ahead and use this technique".

(Now, take two deep breaths and use this technique and relax). Initiate trance induction, install ideomoter signaling. Have client do arm lift test to verify trance depth.

"I want you to become aware of the part of your subconscious that allows you to smoke" (Pause).

If that part of your subconscious does not object, I would like to communicate with that part. Please have that part of your subconscious signify it is okay by raising the index finger on your right hand. If it is not okay, please lift the index finger on your left hand (Thank the part). I would like to now communicate with the part of your subconscious that allows you to smoke and find out what the payoff for smoking is. I know that it is used as a positive tool". (Pause)

If the subconscious has problems finding one, give examples: Stress, socialize, gratification, to feel good, friend.

"I would now like the subconscious part to generate at least three new healthy alternatives to smoking" (Pause).

Examples might be: Read, knit, exercise, self-hypnosis, identify with someone whom you admire and doesn't smoke.

When alternatives are found, ask the subconscious if these alternatives are acceptable, and do they seem and feel acceptable?

If no, go back to the subconscious and identify new alternatives that would be acceptable.

"For this next intervention I will need your permission to touch your shoulder. I want you to allow your mind to go to your favorite place to smoke, where you experience all the feelings and gratifications you get when you smoke (Pause). Now let your mind go to a time when you knew you were in complete control of a situation. You had all the answers and every thing you did was right (Pause). Imagine that you are experiencing it again. Pay attention to all you saw, felt, and words that you heard and the way you talked to yourself (Pause). When you see that the person has achieved this, touch his shoulder for 15 seconds". I want you to now drift back to your favorite situation in which you liked to smoke and to experience being in control again of this situation and say no (Pause). When the client acknowledges they have said no, touch them again on the shoulder for 15 seconds. "I would like you to imagine a situation that occurs two weeks from now when you would have smoked. How does it feel to be a non-smoker? Your subconscious has all the tools you'll need. It has all the dials to tune in whatever is nice for you and to tune out what you don't need to hear or listen to. Your subconscious has so much data, everything you have seen and heard and felt in your life is stored there. It is all there just as data to put together for whatever new ways of perceiving and experiencing". (Terminate)

STOP SMOKING, REFRAMED

This is one of the longest stop smoking interventions available. While longer, it usually produces better results. It is also important to have your patient surrender their cigarettes and matches before beginning the intervention. You must also bear in mind that you need to work within the patient's model of the world.

1. Interview with the client: Assess the client's motivation for wanting to stop smoking. Is the client wanting to stop smoking because of the influence of others, or for himself? Have the client clearly establish what the positive and negative influences surrounding his smoking of cigarettes are (Have client surrender their cigarettes and lighter to you, no exceptions!).

2. Induce trance: Using a suitable technique, induce trance and deepen to the state of somnambulism. Now take the client through the six step refraining process. Once completed, future pace the client and have them see themselves as a nonsmoker. Spend at least five minutes on this, having the client see himself as a non-smoker in cigarette smoking situations, and ask him how they will handle the situations.

3. Bring the client up from trance and ask the client to share how he felt about the total experience. If possible, have the client return for two more sessions in the next four days. This will allow you to reinforce this technique or utilize a different one.

Another thought on stop smoking interventions is to employ the use of a grieving situation in trance. This would allow the patient to say good-bye to his old friend, cigarettes. For many patients their cigarettes have been with them through the good times and the bad times, even when others have failed them.

SMOKING ABATEMENT

You are a very busy person, and so am I. You have lots of things to do now (name), before time comes to an end. Because there is so much to do, you must buy the extra time now. When one has much they want to do, and a way to do, (name), buy this time to do it all, at a very inexpensive price, it would be foolish not to do so, wouldn't it (name). One can find relaxation and happiness in experiencing many new and different aspects of life, friends and family. It's so comforting, to know that there are people who care about and enjoy us. A different stroke for different folks is an old saying. Some people like red, and others like blue. Some people like vanilla, and some people hate it. Some people think that to be sociable they must do as their friends do. If your friends drank poison, could you see yourself being sociable by drinking it too? If your friends shot up with dangerous drugs, could you see yourself being sociable by shooting up too ? If your friends jumped in front of a freight train, could you see yourself being sociable by jumping too? Is that the way to be sociable? If your friends inhaled killer poisonous fumes from the end of a little round tube, could you see yourself being sociable by inhaling those fumes too? Isn't it time to buy time by changing ideas. It's an easy price to pay for the time needed to do all one wants to do, and don't you think that relaxation and comfort is derived from talk and companionship and trying new experiences? And don't you think that true happiness is doing what is best for the self, regardless of what others are doing? Buying that extra time is easy and cheap. If one were drinking poison to be sociable, wouldn't one, to buy extra time quit now, (name). And if one were shooting up with drugs to be sociable, wouldn't one, to buy extra time quit now. And since one was inhaling killer poisonous fumes from a little round tube, hasn't one, quit now. Because now one has easily bought and paid for that extra time, all that is needed and wanted to do the lots there is to do. Now one can walk again, now one can breathe again, and one can, enjoy the relaxing comfort of a healthy life, just because of a, change of ideas now, (name). one can feel relaxed while walking and feel relaxed while talking, and feel at ease while socializing, without poison, even if our friends are poisoning themselves. because we've begun to care about ourselves, because, we are # 1, and we matter most and extra time was bought.

Non-Smoking Direct Intervention

For use with any patient who wants to stop smoking for their own personal benefit. Some honest self motivation must be present. Start the script at a medium level of trance and continue to pace their breathing throughout the intervention.

As you are relaxing deeper and deeper, reflect for a moment on all the success you have already had in the past, the many positive goals that you have already reached and achieved, and feel proud, proud of yourself, proud of all the positive aspects of your life, your creativity, your intelligence. Feel proud of yourself, and know without a doubt that because you have been successful in the past, and because you have reached so many positive goals, you will continue to be successful in every area of your life, every area of your life...you are now more motivated and more determined than ever before to reject all that is unhealthy and harmful to you, Bad habits, tension, stress, the habit of smoking cigarettes...you now reject this habit of smoking cigarettes. You have all the right reasons to be a nonsmoker. You do it for yourself, for your health and well being and that feels fine, very fine. Since you have been successful in the past, you will simply continue to be successful and reach every positive goal that you have, and you now choose to be a nonsmoker. You begin to feel and see an image of yourself without a cigarette or a pack near you. See yourself as a nonsmoker, you are a nonsmoker and that feels fine...you reject the habit of smoking, your mind rejects it and your body rejects it...image throwing a pack of cigarettes out the window and away from you, and that feels great...you have made up your mind, you have made the choice to be a nonsmoker and that feels fine...your body now rejects smoking cigarettes, your lungs no longer have those poisonous fumes in them. They now want to become clean and clear and healthy once again. Your sinuses want to feel clean fresh air. The smell of cigarettes is now disgusting, and the taste is unappealing and unappetizing. Your mouth is clear of smoke, without any trace of cigarette taste, and it feels fresh. Your taste buds experience the appetizing fresh tastes of your food. there are no poisonous and unhealthy fumes in your system...you now choose to be healthy, to be strong, to breathe clean air with your lungs clean and fresh. You have all the right reasons to be a nonsmoker, and you have made up your mind and are now more motivated than ever before to continue to create the most healthy, the most healthy and positive life for yourself, and you are now a nonsmoker, you feel it within. You make a conscious choice not to smoke that cigarette and emotionally you feel just fine. You are a nonsmoker, a nonsmoker, and a positive feeling will stay with you throughout the day, wherever you go. Imagine your daily routine, what would you normally be doing, and see yourself doing these routines all without a cigarette, and feeling fine. You now have a new way of dealing with your old habits. When you are at social events you will join the nonsmokers and start a conversation with someone you have not met before. This is one new way to deal with an old habit, and it is a successful way. It works and you feel fine, just fine, imagine your daily routine without a cigarette and there is a smile on your face, and you feel just fine. Whatever your destination may be, see yourself going there in your usual manner without a cigarette, breathing clean, fresh air, enjoying being a nonsmoker. Continue to see yourself go through the routine of your day, feeling calm, feeling as calm and relaxed as you feel right now. There is a smile on your face, you are a nonsmoker and it feels wonderful, you have stopped smoking cigarettes. You consciously decide not to have a cigarette, and your emotions are fine. It feels fine to be a nonsmoker. Imagine yourself going through a typical day without a cigarette and it feels great. The less you smoke, the better you feel. Soon you will begin to notice that every aspect of your life begins to improve more and more, every day and every night. You will breathe more easily and regain a new healthy vital energy. You are a nonsmoker and that feels fine, see yourself in a situation, enjoying yourself, feeling great without a cigarette, and that feels fine.

(Terminate trance or continue to reinforce what it feels like to be a nonsmoker)

AUTO SUGGESTION
(SELF-HYPNOSIS)

The suggestion is actually the sole agent of hypnosis and the exclusive means of behavior modification. When a person suggests thoughts and ideas to themselves, they have already reasoned them out and has faith in them. Even in hetro-hypnosis the suggestions of the hypnotist do not take effect without the unconscious agreement of the subject.

We know that whenever there is a clash between the conscious and unconscious minds, it is the unconscious mind that wins out. Therefore, for a suggestion to be carried out by the conscious mind, acceptance by the unconscious mind is necessary. It follows that auto-suggestion is usually much more meaningful than suggestions administered by someone else, moreover, when a person gives suggestions to himself he will, in fact, participate directly and more actively in his behavior modification goals than when induced to do so by another person.

The most effective method of auto-suggestion is probably a combination of pre-hypnotic and pictorial suggestions. The person will word his suggestion after meeting the preparatory conditions, and before self-hypnosis. When he has achieved self-hypnosis, his visual image will reflect his suggestion.

In conveying suggestions to the unconscious mind, picture images seem to be more effective than words. This is because the unconscious mind understands pictures better than words. A picture is, indeed, worth a thousand words.

If the patient can visualize himself doing a certain behavior or accomplishing something, then he becomes fully capable of accomplishing that scene. Normally it is not too difficult for the patient to visualize himself doing a certain behavior, as it usually is a behavior that at some point in their past was a normal behavior for him. Some patients may need to struggle harder than others to put together a picture(s) of themselves doing that desired behavior, but if you encourage them to endure the struggle the payoff will be well worth the effort. Your encouragement will be most instrumental in their beginning.

RULES OF AUTO SUGGESTION

For auto-suggestions to be more effective, a number of rules should be followed:

1. Suggestions should be condensed, revised, and perfected on a piece of paper and read several times prior to the induction of self-hypnosis.

2. Auto-suggestions should be direct, permissive, and positive. Negative words and phrases such as not", can't", "won't", should be avoided. Example (for a headache): "Upon awakening, my headache will be gone." it would be better to suggest, My head is feeling clear and better, I am becoming more and more comfortable and tranquil in every way." Another advantage of applying this procedure is that the unconscious mind will be given sufficient time to assimilate the idea.

3. The suggestion should be combined with a motive that enhances the effectiveness of the suggestion. This may be done through visual imagery. Example, When a person gives himself a suggestion to overcome tension at the time of a job interview he may envision getting a good, prestigious job instead of saying to himself not to be nervous and tense during the interview.

4. Suggestions should be given singularly. The unconscious mind cannot deal with more than one idea at a time. Additionally, the

suggestion should be repeated and reinforced in successive hypnotic sessions until the desired goal is achieved.

5. Auto-suggestions should be positively and logically worded and capable of being fulfilled.

In summation, the suggestion needs to be positive, short (one to three sentences), and linked to a positive mental image as a point of reference for the patient's subconscious. Self-hypnosis can be done several times during an average day, but remember to deal with only one issue per trance to gain the maximum effectiveness of self-hypnosis. It is acceptable to do three separate self-hypnotic inductions and deal with three separate issues.

DEEPENING PROCEDURES FOR SELF-HYPNOSIS

Although light to deep trance have the same effect, for the unconscious mind to assimilate the auto-suggestion and to deepen auto-hypnosis, a number of techniques can be applied, some of which are common to hetro-hypnosis.

Visual Imagery Technique: This is one of the best techniques for deepening self-hypnosis. You imagine yourself in any situation that gives you peace and serenity. For instance, you may see yourself lying down comfortably in your bed, enjoying a sound sleep and pleasant dreams; or you may be lying in a hammock, or lying on a beach and watching the ocean waves, or any similar relaxing imagery, "as you imagine drifting deeper into relaxation".

Escalator Technique: You may imagine yourself riding down an escalator. Then you start counting slowly to yourself from twenty to zero. You should think to yourself that the further the escalator goes down, the deeper you go into hypnosis. Also, between each number you may imagine yourself drifting deeper into relaxation.

Counting Method: You may count from 100 forwards or backwards, and by one's, two's, three's, four's, etc. With every count you should imagine yourself drifting deeper and deeper into relaxation. Deepening self-hypnosis requires the same kind of practice or conditioning as the induction of hypnosis. therefore, with every count, you should coordinate your bodily functioning with your thoughts. For instance, you should designate a particular number by which time you feel your mind is separated from your body.

Hand Levitation Method: You may suggest hand levitation to yourself and imagine that when your fingers touch your face, your arm will immediately become heavy and fall to your thigh. As this happens, you will go deeper into hypnosis than ever before.

Post-Hypnotic Suggestion: As with hetro-hypnosis, each time you hypnotize yourself you can give the suggestion that the next time you attempt self-hypnosis you will go more quickly and more deeply into the hypnotic state.

Deepening self-hypnosis can also be assisted by making a cassette audio-tape.

WAKING FROM SELF-HYPNOSIS

To awaken from self-hypnosis, (or more properly termed, to return to one's normal state of awareness), all you have to do is to suggest that you are going to do just that. this can be done in several ways;

1. Suggest to yourself that on the count of three you will be wide awake, refreshed, and full of energy. Envision the face of a clock set at the time you wish to awaken.

2. Think about the length of time you wish to remain in trance (this should be done prior to self-hypnosis), and the specific time you wish to wake up.

When you first start practicing self-hypnosis, you may drop off into a natural sleep. to avoid this, you can suggest to yourself that you will count back from 0 to 20, and at the count of 20 you will be in trance. once you have achieved the hypnotic state, and after you have accomplished auto-suggestion, you should count from 1 to 5, and at the count of 5 you will wake up.

When you are about to wake up, always suggest to yourself that upon awaking, you will feel relaxed, refreshed, clearheaded, full of energy, and happy.

TESTS OF SELF-HYPNOSIS

To recognize whether you are self-hypnotized, and if so, to what depth, you may give yourself a number of tests. It is best not to attempt giving any test to yourself or attempt to produce any hypnotic phenomena until you have practiced self-hypnosis successfully several times. However, when you are sure of achieving the state of self-hypnosis, then you can give relevant tests to yourself. If you respond properly to the tests, then you know you are self-hypnotized. Tests of self-hypnosis are very similar to the hetro-hypnotic depth tests. The only difference between self-hypnosis tests and hetro-hypnosis depth tests is that in the latter the hypnotist gives you the tests, but in the former, the tests are self managed.

Eye Catalepsy Test: After having achieved relaxation and eye closure, suggest to yourself that your eyelids are getting very heavy and that they are locked together. You may word your suggestion like this: One, my eyes are locked together. Two, my eyelids are actually so glued that it will be an enormous task to move them. Three, they are stuck fast, tight, very tight. As you mention the word tight, preferably mentally, try to open them, but stop trying as soon as you are unable to do so. When you respond in satisfactory manner to the test suggestion, give yourself the following suggestion and continue on with the induction procedure: Now my eyes are perfectly normal in every way, and I can open them whenever I choose, but I will keep them closed for the remainder of the induction. I am now going even deeper into self-hypnosis. If you respond properly to this test, then you can be sure that you are hypnotized.

Arm Catalepsy Test: Levitate one of your hands and suggest to yourself that it is getting rigid and taut, and you cannot bring it down again. After you respond successfully to this test, suggest to yourself that your arm has become loose and limp and is going to drop to your thigh. Include in your suggestion the idea that when your hand touches your thigh you will go to an even deeper state of hypnosis. Another variation of this test is that you suggest to yourself that your hand is getting very heavy, that it is stuck to the arm of the chair, and that you can not move it or lift it up.

Hand Levitation Test: Imagine that one of your hands is beginning to lose all sensation of weight, and it is becoming buoyant. At the count of three, your rising fingers will touch your face (suggest to yourself that this will be done involuntarily and without conscious effort). After your fingers have touched your face, let your arm drop on your lap and imagine that upon dropping your hand on your thigh, you will develop a much deeper state of hypnosis.

Foot Test: The test can be accomplished while sitting or lying down. First, you imagine that one of your feet is very heavy. You imagine that your foot is so heavy that it is stuck to the floor and you are unable to move it or raise it. The harder you try to raise your foot, the less you will be able to do it.

Glove Anesthesia Test: You can give glove anesthesia suggestions to yourself. To produce glove anesthesia, you should rub the back of one of your hands clockwise or counter clockwise, and suggest to yourself that by rubbing your hand it becomes numb, senseless, and wooden-like. You will lose all sensation in that hand and you will feel no pain if the hand is stimulated. You may also suggest to yourself that numbness will develop in your hand simultaneously with hand levitation, and will remain in your hand until a certain period of time after awakening. Wording of the suggestion should be something like this: Upon awakening, my hand will be numb, cold and senseless for one minute. When anesthesia is affected in your hand, you will feel a little pressure on the spot that you choose to pinch, but no pain.

If you succeed in passing these tests, you can be sure that you have developed at least a medium state of hypnosis. As you keep practicing, a greater depth of hypnosis will be produced.

SPIEGEL'S TEST

This is another method of how to teach patients to hypnotize themselves and reinforce their therapeutic suggestions. This technique was devolved by two brothers who were psychiatrists, Herbert and David Spiegel.

You should advise your patients to do the following: Sit or lie down, and to yourself, count to three. At one, you do one thing, at two, you do two things, at three, you do three things. In all, you carry out six things. At one, look up towards your eyebrows; at two, while looking up, close your eyelids and take a deep breath, at three exhale, let your eyes relax, and let your body float.

As you feel yourself floating, you permit one hand or the other to feel like a buoyant balloon and let it float upwards. When it reaches this upright position, it becomes a signal for you to enter a state of meditation.

This floating sensation signals your mind to turn inward and pay attention to your own thoughts, like private meditation Ballet dancers and athletes float all the time. That is why they concentrate and coordinate their movements so well. When they do not float they are tense and do not do as well.

Then the Spiegels advise their patients that in the beginning they should do these exercises as often as ten different times a day, preferably every one or two hours. At first the exercise takes a minute, but as the patient becomes more experienced, he can do it in much less time.

According to the Spiegels, the patient, to de-hypnotize himself, should count backwards in this manner; Now three, get ready, two, with your eyelids closed, roll up your eyes, and one, let your eyelids open slowly. Then when your eyes are back in focus, slowly make a fist with the hand that is up, and as you open your fist slowly, your usual sensation and control returns, let your hand float downwards.

This is a version that requires practice several times over to master.

SUBJECTIVE TECHNIQUE

Sit in a comfortable chair or lie down on a couch or bed. Fix your eyes on a spot on the wall above eye level or on the ceiling. Try to meet all the prepertory requirements for self-hypnosis. Then focus your attention on your eyelids during the procedure while thinking of the symbol "55".

Now, first imagine that your eyelids are becoming very heavy. Try to feel this heaviness. Again and again tell yourself mentally; "my eyes are getting very heavy". I feel my eyes getting very heavy, and the heavier they become, the more comfortable and relaxed I feel. It seems that it is impossible for me to keep my eyelids open. It really feels so good to close my eyes. I am going count to three. When I complete the count, it will be absolutely impossible for me to keep my eyes open. One...my eyes are narrowing to a slit, they are about to close. Two.... my eyelids are going to drop involuntarily. Three...they are closing they are closing...they are closing. Now tell yourself "My eyelids are now locked together, they are stuck fast, so tightly that I can not open them. now, do not try any longer.... I can open my eyes when ever I choose, but will keep them closed for the remainder of the induction." Now think of a peaceful scene, imagine you are walking around a swimming pool in the middle of a beautiful garden. It is spring, the weather is very pleasant. It is 3 o'clock in the afternoon, you keep walking alongside the pool. All around the pool are red, white and yellow roses. Alongside the pool are jasmine trees. A mild breeze blows from the flowers, bringing the sweet smell of roses and jasmine. As you continue walking, the sweet jasmine scent stays with you. Suddenly, a few yards from the pool, you see a hammock stretched between two shady trees. You decide to lie down in that hammock in the midst of the beautiful garden and enjoy a deep relaxation. So you approach the hammock, you lie down in it, and find it very comfortable and relaxing. You feel relaxed and comfortable that ten minutes of actual time pass like one minute. As you enjoy your relaxed state, a pretty bird lands on the branch of a tree in front of you. You keep looking at it. After a few seconds the bird leaves its perch and starts to fly toward you. It is getting closer and closer to you. You wish to follow the movements of the bird, but the beauty of the scene causes you to close your eyes and go into a very deep sleep.

This imagery may work as a very pleasant method of induction and take you into a deep hypnotic trance. Any variation of this scene which suits individual needs can be applied for the induction of self-hypnosis. You may even tape a scene like the above, and listen to it daily.

COMBINATION INDUCTION

Seat yourself in a comfortable chair with your feet flat on the floor, your legs extended, and your hands on your thighs or on the arms of the chair. Meet the preparatory rules for self-hypnosis. Fix your gaze on something above eye level.

Begin counting slowly from 1 to 10. Say the number one, direct your attention on your eyes and tell yourself repeatedly, "My eyes are getting heavy, very heavy. I feel my eyes becoming so heavy that at the count of 3 I will not be able to keep them open, they will close automatically". Count to two and think of the symbol "55". Roll your eyes up into the back of your head, then count to three and tell yourself, "My eyelids are so heavy now that I cannot open them. It is just as if they were glued together.... I will now go deeper into self-relaxation. I am able to open my eyes whenever I choose, but I will keep them closed for the remainder of the induction. Next, count to 4, think of the symbol "55", and give yourself the following suggestions; "my toes, feet, calves, and legs are getting very heavy. I feel a tingling sensation all over my legs, it feels very nice. both my legs, from my toes up to the pelvic area feel stuck to the floor.... I now go even deeper into self-relaxation. I am able to move my legs whenever I choose, and I now will go even deeper into self-relaxation. Now, count to 5, think of the "55" and say to yourself; I feel my abdominal muscles becoming numb and heavy. Even the pit of my stomach is becoming wooden-like and relaxed. Count to 6, think of the image "55", and continue telling yourself; "Now I can feel the muscles in my chest becoming relaxed, I am breathing more regularly and more easily.... (then thinking now and then of the symbol "55", continue counting and with the count of 7, tell yourself): "Now I feel a numb, wooden-like sensation

96

in my fingers, wrists, hands, arms and forearms. my arms feel just as though I have been sleeping on them. Eight, the muscles of my neck and my entire body, from my neck down are relaxed. Nine, I feel my facial muscles becoming loose. My head is also very heavy and at the same time very relaxed and refreshed...my whole body feels loose and limp, from the top of my head right down to my toes......with every breath I take, I can feel myself drifting into a deeper and deeper state of relaxation. Then you have to visualize a relaxed and pleasant scene like the one described in the "subjective technique". it can be some pleasant scene you imagine in the future. It can be a peaceful, mountainous scene, a blue sky with one or two billowy clouds moving slowly. On a lake with a sailboat floating gently, or any scene that makes you feel good, drowsy, and relaxed.

The "key word" and suggestions should be given at the appropriate time. The more practice you put into this procedure will be directly reflected in the outcome you achieve. this would be an excellent script to record on a cassette for your personal use.

DEEP MUSCLE RELAXATION TRAINING

This is phase one of three phases. The muscle relaxation phase and guided imagery phase follows this script and should be taught in this order. This is particularly good for your patients who have trouble relaxing.

The number of seconds to pause is denoted by the number in parentisis (0).

Welcome to this session. During the next 30 minutes we will work our way through deep muscle relaxation training. The end result of this session is for you to have a heightened sense of awareness of what your body feels like to be fully relaxed. This technique alone will not teach you every thing you need to know. It is imperative that you practice all three phases of this program.

We will begin by having you assume a comfortable position. You can either be sitting down in a chair or laying down. If you use a chair, try to make it one with arms, if laying down, do not use a pillow. If your clothing is too tight and uncomfortable, loosen it slightly now (4). Settle back now as comfortable as you can (4). Focus your attention on my voice (3). As other thoughts drift into your mind, let them drift away and continue to focus on my voice only (4). (spend four minutes talking the client through a deep breathing exercise). As you relax, clench your right fist, now clench your fist tighter and tighter, and study the tension in your right fist and forearm. You can feel the tension become uncomfortable in your right fist and forearm. You can feel the tension become uncomfortable in your right fist as you keep it tightly clenched (3). Now relax (4). Let the fingers of your right hand become loose (5). Observe the contrast in the feelings of your right hand (5). Let yourself go and try to become more relaxed all over (5). Once more again, clench your right fist really

98

tight (3). Hold it tight (3). Now notice the tension again, it feels very tight and uncomfortable (2). Now let go (2). Relax, straighten out your fingers (3). Notice the difference once more (10). Now we will repeat that with your left hand and forearm (2). Clench your left fist while the rest of your body relaxes (3). Clench your fist tight and feel the tension (3). Now relax (5). Again, enjoy the contrast in feelings (4). Let your mind focus on that feeling of relaxation. Repeat that once more, clench your left fist (3). Make your fist very tight and tense (3). Now relax and feel the difference (4). Slowly straighten out your fingers (10). Clench both fists now (3). Tight, and tighter (2). Both fists tense, forearms tense, study the sensation (2). Relax now (2). Let the feelings of relaxation flow into both hands (2). Straighten out your fingers and feel the relaxation (3). Continue relaxing your hands and forearms more and more (3) Now bend both your elbows and tense your biceps by pulling your hands towards your shoulders (3). Tense, them tighter and study the feelings of tension (5). Now straighten out your arms (4). Let them relax, and now feel the difference again (3). Let the relaxation develop (8). Once more, tense your biceps (4). Hold that tension and observe it carefully (4). Straighten your arms and allow the feelings of relaxation to flow into yours arms (4). rRelax to the best of your ability (8). Now straighten your arms so that you feel the most tension in the triceps muscle along the back of your arms (3). Now relax (5). Move your arms back into a comfortable position (5). Let the relaxation flow on its own accord (8). 'your arms should feel comfortably heavy as you allow the relaxation to flow (5). Once more, straighten your arms so that you feel the tension in your triceps (8). Let your arms relax again and focus on the comfortable heavy feeling of relaxation in your arms (6). Now let's focus on pure relaxation in the arms without any tension. Move your arms into a comfortable position and let them relax (8). Let the relaxation flow into your arms (3). Focus on that nice warm feeling in your arms (10). even when your arms seem fully relaxed, try to let your arms achieve a deeper level of relaxation (12). Now we will move upwards to the head and shoulders (2). We will start by letting all your muscles go loose and heavy. Just settle back quietly and comfortably. Wrinkle up your forehead now (3), wrinkle it tighter (5). Now stop wrinkling your forehead (4). Relax and allow it to smooth out (3). Picture your entire forehead and scalp becoming smoother as the relaxation increases (10). Now frown and crease your brows and study the tension (6). Let go of the tension once again, smooth out your forehead once more (10). Now close your eyes tighter and tighter (5), feel the tension (3). Now relax your eyes (4). Keep your eyes closed gently, comfortably and notice the relaxation (10). Now clench your jaws (10). Relax your jaws now, let your lips part slightly (6). Appreciate the feeling of relaxation (12). Now press your tongue hard against the roof of your mouth (4). Look for the tension (4). All right, let your tongue return to a comfortable and relaxed position (10). Now press your lips together (4), tighter and tighter (4). Relax your lips, note the contrast between tension and relaxation (8). Feel the relaxation all over your face (8). Now to attend to your neck muscles, press your head back as far as it can go and feel the tension in your neck (3). Roll it to the right and feel the tension shift (3), now roll it to the left (3). Straighten your head and bring it forward (3). Press your chin against your chest (4). Let your head return to a comfortable position, and study the relaxation (5). Let the relaxation develop (10). Now shrug your shoulders straight up (4), hold the tension (4). Drop your shoulders slowly and feel the relaxation (4). Feel your neck and shoulders relaxing (8). Shrug your shoulders up and forward (4), now back, feel the tension in your shoulders and in your upper back (4). Drop your shoulders slowly once more and relax (6). Let the relaxation spread deeply into your shoulders, right into your back muscles (6). Relax your neck and throat, and your jaw and other facial areas as the pure relaxation takes over and goes deeper (3), deeper, even deeper (10). Allow yourself to focus on the warm, heavy comfortable feeling in your face and shoulders (12). If other thoughts drift into your mind, let them drift on by and continue to focus on my voice (8). We now shift our focus to the trunk of your body, start with relaxing your entire body to the best of your ability (8). Feel that comfortable heaviness that accompanies relaxation (8). Breathe easily and freely, in and out (5). Notice how the relaxation increases as you exhale (10). As you breathe out, feel that relaxation (4). Now breathe in and fill up your lungs, inhale deeply and hold your breath (4). Study the sensation (3). Now exhale, let the walls of your chest grow loose and push the air out automatically (3). Continue relaxing and breathe freely and gently (6). Feel the relaxation and enjoy it (8). With the rest of your body as relaxed as possible, fill your lungs again (8). That's fine, breath out, and again, breathe in deeply and hold it (8), now breathe out and appreciate the relief (4). Just breathe normally (6). Continuing relaxing your chest and let the relaxation spread to your back (6). To your shoulders (6), to your neck (6), to your arms (6). Merely let go and enjoy the relaxation (12). Now let's pay attention to your abdominal muscles, pull your stomach in (3). Pull the muscles right in and feel the tension this way (6). Now relax again, let your stomach out. Continue to breathe normally and easily and feel the gentle massaging action all over your chest and stomach (12). Now pull your stomach in again and hold the tension (8). Release the tension (8). Once more pull in your stomach fully and feel the tension (8). Now relax your stomach fully (3). Let the tension dissolve as the relaxation grows deeper (6). Each time you breathe out notice the rhythmic relaxation both in your lungs and in your stomach (10). Notice how your chest and stomach relaxes more and more (8). Try and let go of all the muscle tension anywhere in your body (12). Now direct your attention to your lower back (3). Arch up your back, make your lower back quite hollow, and feel the tension along your spine (4). Now settle back comfortably again, relaxing the lower back (10). Arch your back up again and feel the tension as you do so. Try to keep the rest of your body relaxed as possible. Try to localize the tension throughout your lower back area (2). Relax once more (3). Relax your upper back (6). Spread the relaxation to your stomach (6). Now to your chest (6). Now to your shoulders (6). Now to your arms (6). Now to your facial area (6). These parts are relaxing further and further, and further and even deeper (6). Let it flow as a warm, heavy, comfortable feeling (12). Let go of all tensions and just relax (8). now flex your buttocks and thighs. Flex your thighs by pressing down your heels as hard as you can (6). Relax and note the difference (8). Straighten your knees and flex your thigh muscles again, hold the tension (6). Relax your hips and thighs (8). Allow the relaxation to proceed on its own (10). Press your feet and toes downwards, away from your face, so that calf muscles become tense, study that tension (6). Relax your feet and calves (8). This time, bend your feet away from your face so that you feel tension along your shins (6), bring your toes back up (2), relax again. (6) keep relaxing for awhile (6),now let yourself relax further all over (6). Relax your feet (6). Relax your ankles now (6). Relax your calves now (6). Relax your shins now (6). Relax your knees now (6). Relax your thighs now (6). Relax your buttocks now (6). Relax your hips now (6). Feel the heaviness of your lower body as you realize still further (8). Let go now, more and more (4). Feel that relaxation all over. Let it proceed to your upper back (6). Keep realizing more and more deeply (12). Make sure that no tension has crept into your throat (2). Relax your neck and your jaws and all your facial muscles (4). Keep relaxing your whole body like that for a while. Let yourself totally relax (12). Now you can become twice as relaxed by taking in a really deep breath and slowly exhaling (6). Close your eyes so that you become less aware of objects and movements around you, and prevent any surface tensions from developing (8). Breath in deeply and feel yourself becoming heavier (6). Take a long deep breath and let it out very slowly (6). Feel how heavy and relaxed you have become (12). The relaxation is flowing thru you in a warm and comfortable way (30). In a state of perfect relaxation you should feel unwilling to move a single muscle in your body (3). Think about the effort that would be required to raise your right arm, as you think about raising your right arm, see if you can notice any tensions that might have crept into your right shoulder and your arm (6). Now you decide not to lift your arm, but to continue relaxing (12). Observe the relief and the disappearance of the tension (6). Just continue relaxing like that (12). When you wish to get up, count backward from five to one (6).

You should then feel fine and refreshed, wide-awake and clam, slowly open your eyes and look about (4). Flex your fingers and toes slightly. Now in a slow and easy manner you can bring yourself to your feet (6). It maybe necessary for you to repeat this exercise several times to develop a strong sense of awareness of what your body feels like to be relaxed. The value of this exercise is for you to develop a heightened sense of awareness of the feelings of relaxation, and the feelings of tension.

Muscle Relaxation Script

Welcome to the second in a series of your relaxation training. Before moving into the second phase of this program lets take a minute to review the first phase. Hopefully by now you have repeated the first phase of relaxation and tension.

During this phase I want you to mentally recall the feelings you experienced during the first session. Recall them slowly (10). Tighten and loosen your muscles if needed to re-awaken the feeling of relaxation (10). Settle back, and make yourself comfortable (15). Also recall the breathing exercises now that we are prepared (15). Lets move on (5). Begin with your feet, focus on your toes and feet, focus on that comfortable, warm, heavy feeling (10). If you find distracting thoughts drift into your mind, let them drift on by, don't try to force the thoughts out of your mind (3). Just let them drift on by (10). Focus now on the calves of your legs (10). Feel them grow heavier and heavier (10). Feel the tension drift away and that heavy comfortable feeling flow in (15). Now let that nice feeling of relaxation flow slowly upwards (15). You can feel it slowly working into your thighs (10). You're now feeling that nice warm heavy feeling spread throughout your thighs (10). Feel your thigh grow heavier and heavier (10). Feel the tension drift away and that heavy comfortable feeling flow freely (15). If you find distracting thoughts coming into your mind, let them drift on by and continue to focus on my voice (15). Let that comfortable feeling move upwards into your hips and buttocks (10). Let that mental image become warm and heavy, very comfortable (15). The feeling is becoming very soothing and relaxing (15). The feeling becomes more and more comfortable as the tension drifts away (20). Now feel that comfortable feeling move up into your stomach and lower back (10). Feel the tension start slowly drift away (10). That comfortable feeling of relaxation is starting to flow in and feels so soothing and warm (10). The feeling of relaxation continues to grow and feel warmer and more comfortable (10). Don't hesitate to let your body relax and sink into a wonderful feeling of relaxation (15). It is now traveling upwards again, into your chest and shoulders (8). The tension is now flowing away (10). The tension still slowly drifting (10). The feeling of relaxation is now taking over in your chest and shoulders (15). Spreading so slowly, and very relaxing (20). The feeling of relaxation becomes deeper and deeper (25). Now the feeling of relaxation is seeping down through your arms and into your hands (15). Now you feel your arms and hands grow warm and heavy (12). That heavy comfortable feeling is becoming more and more soothing (12). The tension has drifted out of arms and hands now, and the warm heavy feeling is flowing freely (10). Your arms and hands continue to grow warm and heavy (10). Let the feeling of relaxation go deeper and deeper (20). Now let your mind slowly move to focus on your neck and scalp (15). Let the warm comfortable feeling spread up through your neck and into your scalp (10). The tension is slowly drifting away (12). Now the warm comfortable feeling is flowing and feeling better and better (12). Slowly you feel the warmth move you deeper and deeper into relaxation (15). The feeling of relaxation is now drifting down into your facial muscles (10). the tension is drifting out now and that warm relaxed feeling is increasing (15). Now the warm heavy comfortable feeling if flowing with warmth and comfort (30). Now you are feeling that warm, heavy, comfortable feeling engulf your entire body (45). The feeling flows so freely into the warm wonderful feeling of relaxation (60). Now, very slowly count backwards from five to one (10). Now slowly move your toes (5). Now also move your fingers slightly (5). Open your eyes and slowly look about you (4). At this time you will start to feel more alert and refreshed (6). You may feel free to get up now and move about. it is recommended that you practice this technique several times before moving on to the guided imagery phase.

GUIDED IMAGERY

During this session we will focus on guided imagery as a means of relaxation. This is the third and final teaching phase in progressive relaxation techniques. We start this session with a reflective look back to the sessions of deep muscle techniques and muscle relaxation. Try to recall in your mind the feelings you experienced during these exercises. The bold (0) denote pauses in seconds.

Assume a comfortable position before you begin to form the mental image of your body relaxing (6). Loosen any tight clothing and let the warm comfortable feeling of relaxation take over (12). If any distracting thoughts enter your mind, let them drift on bye and continue to focus on the sound of my voice, and that warm, heavy and comfortable feeling that is starting to move through your body (15). If you have trouble recalling that feeling of relaxation at this time, stop briefly and perform phase one again of the deep muscle relaxation technique until you have developed a re-awareness of relaxation in your body (15). Now mentally recreate that feeling of relaxation in your body (10). let it begin with your toes (10). slowly, that warm comfortable feeling starts moving upwards (10). Now moving into the calves of your legs (10). The warm heavy feeling is flowing stronger, but quite easily (15). The feeling now moves into your thighs (10). Slowly and very warmly spreading (10). That warm comfortable feeling is now moving into your hips and buttocks (10). Slowly and warmly the feeling of relaxation is spreading throughout your lower body (10). Feel the warmth and comfort spread to your stomach and lower back (10). Feel those muscles gently let go and the relaxation flow in (15). The warm feeling of comfort is now spreading upwards through your chest and shoulders (10). Progressing gently and slowly onwards up through your neck and scalp (15). Take a minute now to dwell on the feeling you are experiencing in your body. (Sixty second pause) Now that you have achieved a state of relaxation, continue to focus on my voice as we create a mental picture in your mind (10). Imagine yourself now, sitting down and leaning against a huge tree in an open field (15). You are sitting in lush, soft green grass (15). You can feel a gentle warm breeze (10). The breeze is soft and warm on your face (15). just like a soft warm caress (15). You feel very relaxed now, deeply relaxed (10). A warm comfortable feeling holds your body and mind in relaxation (15). In your mind's eye you slowly turn and look upwards (5). Looking to the top of the tree filled with leaves (10). You see that warm gentle breeze stirring the leaves on the tree, ever so softly and gently (10). You casually notice that from the top of the tree a leaf has broken away and is starting to fall (10). The warm breeze is cradling the leaf (10). Rocking the leaf gently back and forth (10). The leaf moves ever so slowly in the breeze (10). Feel that warm gentle breeze again, gently touching your face (10). Notice the free flowing relaxation going through your body (15). You also notice that the leaf is still falling ever so slowly (10). It is still being cradled and rocked, back and forth by the gentle warm breeze you feel (15). The leaf is still slowly working its way down in its descent to the ground (15). The leaf is moving so slowly and unhurried (15). Still gently floating and moving so gracefully with the breeze (15). Unhurried or bothered by time, the leaf continues its slow and deliberate descent to the ground (15). Let your mind slowly turn inward to become re-aware of the wonderful state of relaxation your body is enjoying (20). That comfortable, warm heavy feeling continues to flow through out your person (30). Now your mind slowly turns back to the leaf (5). It is still making its graceful descent downwards (15). Still gently swaying in the breeze (10). Back and forth, so slowly and gently, as it moves to its downward destination (15). With slow graceful motion, the warm pleasant breeze you feel is still carrying the leaf further downward (15). You observe the leaf moving with gentle and tender grace (15). The leaf is being cradled by the warm breeze; you can also feel the warmness of your body relaxing, and the gentle warm breeze caressing you (20). The leaf is moving slowly (10). Still making its unhurried descent to the ground below (20). The leaf is coming closer to the ground now (15). Still gently and slowly moving with an air of grace in its every movement (20). At times the leaf will appear almost to be suspended in the air by the gentle nurturing of the warm breeze (20). Now it appears to be in its final, but graceful descent (20). Slowly, with a gentle swaying motion, the leaf comes to rest beside you (10). The leaf, like you, has finally come to a complete state of rest. Mentally, let your mind explore your body in this state of relaxation (60). Now slowly count backwards from five to one (10). Slowly now, open your eyes and look about you (5). Slowly move your toes and fingers, and you will find muscle tension returning (10). To obtain the maximum amount of effectiveness from this session, it is recommended that you repeat this exercise several times over on your own. in time, the mental image of the falling leaf will become your key to unlocking your relaxation through your mind's association with this mental image. You may in the future decide to create your own personal image to better suit your personality. I would recommend you consult with an individual in the field of psychology for assistance and guidance. if you do not desire to seek out consultation, I would suggest you use a serene, calm scene for your mental image, such as a lake, snow covered mountain, etc.

HEALING STARS

This journey/intervention is good for general internal healing. Start reading the script when the patient has been deepened to a medium state.

Imagine a moonlit night with millions of stars. Focus on the brightest star that you see. The star stands out as very special. All of a sudden the star burst into a million pieces and comes showering over you very softly, and you feel comfort, warmth, and peace shine over you. At this time, feel the warmth from the pieces as they blanket around you (Pause). Now visualize many small, bright, white stars breathing in through the bottom of your feet. These stars of healing come up through your legs in a rolling fashion, accumulating more and more stars up into your hips, coming up through your abdomen, hundreds appear, traveling through your chest, shoulders, now through your arms, to your hands, still entering through you feet thousands of soft, soothing, white healing stars now filling your head. You give them permission to heal you, as they begin to fade into your body, which absorbs each and every one. You now focus your attention on your feet, where the process repeats itself. The stars enter again in a swirling motion, coming up through your feet; your legs are filled with hundreds of wonderful stars. They continue onward entering your pelvis, buttocks, back, and chest, accumulating by the thousands. Continuing through your shoulders, arms, hands, back up through your arms, up your throat into your head. This time before they fade away, you take the strongest of the stars; gather them into a ball located on the right side of your stomach area. Gather them all from your head, arms, and legs and send the ball on a reconnaissance mission to an area in your body in which you feel some pain or discomfort and that you would like healed. Let that area absorb hundreds of these stars your willingness to heal that point of your body. Now again on your own, visualize another grouping of stars entering from your feet, filling your entire body (pause). Thousands of white, wonderful, healing, soothing, beams of light illuminate from your glowing white stars. Gather the strongest again in your lower stomach area on the right side. Allow hundreds of strong healing stars to comprise your ball. Send them to the same place or possibly another place, let that spot absorb the strongest healing stars and let them fade into that area.

PEACEFUL VOID

This procedure is designed to help your patients find an inner peace within themselves. Start this script at a medium depth of trance.

Now clear your mind for this journey, imagining that you have inhaled a green cloud, and exhale a leaf falling gently...as you inhale, the rising green cloud floats higher and higher...as you exhale the leaf floats down gently...inhale the rising green cloud...and exhale the gentle falling leaf .. if you cannot see the color, then visualize the word green, look at each letter, g—r—e—e—n. Now see the entire word green. the word green now becomes the color green. Now gently glide green into your heart center. let your heart center accept it and radiate green from it. Allow green to soak into your compassionate heart and make the exchange of love with green. Both become one at this time. Imagine a glowing green light in your heart center that will be with you during this time. Take a few moments now to feel and experience this calming, cooling and soothing green glow as it emanates from your heart center (Pause). Now acknowledge unfilled desires and illusions and fantasy regarding outside people, objects, or addictions. They are something you desire, transform these desires into thoughts. Sink the thoughts down into your chest. Move them out of your mind and into the lower part of your body. Make the thoughts reality in your being. transform the thoughts into transparent particles and bursts of clear energy. Imagine your thoughts one by one transforming into nothingness, into the void. Feel this void in detail, see its shape, size, color, thickness, weight, taste, and smell, feel it again (Pause). Now take the green light of love that has been soaking in your heart center and use it to caress the void. Treat it kindly and affectionately, as you would the outside person or object. Outside material and objects and inside emotions may try from time to time to enter this void. Recognize their importance and gently let them know that the void is a place for nothing, and that they may pass through and vanish, and know they will not disturb the void. Draw the void close to you, hug it, stroke it lovingly, and gently welcome it into your body...allow the void to float within you, it is your friend, it may feel awkward at first, that's okay. Don't try to fill the space. Enjoy the emptiness and joy. just let the void exist and become the love that embraces it. When you feel you have experienced all that is necessary for now, bring yourself back to a conscious state This procedure is best practiced several times, and audiocassette tape would be helpful.

THE VIEW OF LIFE

The purpose of this exercise is to provide the individual and the therapist a better understanding of the individual and how they are oriented to life. This should provide significant insight for the individual into where they are in dealing with life and problems.

Begin with taking the patient down into trance, medium stage would be appropriate.

Tell the patient the following story: (Wherever you find a number in parenthesis, this denotes the recommended pause in seconds before moving on with the script)

Now I want you to picture yourself approaching a wall, this wall can be any size, shape, color or texture that you want it to be. Take time now to notice the wall. What does it look like? What does it feel like? Is it hot or cold? Does it have a smell? (12) Now you must cross the wall, you can use anything you want to cross to the other side, the only thing you can't do is blow-up the wall. (8) Now you find yourself in a nice forest setting, as you stroll down through the forest you can notice the tall trees and pretty flowers along the way. (4) Now you find yourself coming up to a river, you pause there to look at it. This can be a flow of water anywhere, because you have seen this flow of water before. (4) Now is the time for you to prepare for your journey up stream to the source of the water. You can take any thing you want with you on your journey to the source. (6) Now you have started your journey up stream in search of the source. (10) Now you are approaching the source of the water. (4) Now that you are at the source of the water, I want you to closely examine it. (6) Now its time for you to go back down stream. you slowly turn away from the source and start your journey back. (4) Along the way you notice a bit of a beach in front of you, I want you to stop there briefly now that you are on the beach doing whatever you want to do. (12) Now its time for you to leave the beach and continue back down stream. (4) As you continue back down stream you see the place where you started from. (4) Now you step back into the forest and walk back down the path until you see the wall again. (4) Now you are standing in front of the wall again, examine it closely now. (4) As before, you need to go to the other side of the wall now by any means you choose. (6) Now you are standing on the other side of the wall where your journey first begin. now bring the client back up from trance. Check their orientation to ensure that they are out of trance.

Explain the following meanings to them about what they encountered on their journey:

The first wall represents your natural wall of defenses to others in the world around you.

The forest represents nothing, a transition from the wall to the water.

The river/flow of water. This represents your flow of life as you are experiencing it presently.

The source of the river/flow of water represents your very life essence. Your source of energy, motivation, etc.

The beach, what you did on the beach represents your ability to play.

The second wall represents your present defenses in life.

Now have the patient describe their journey in great detail and assist them in understanding the significant points of their journey.

ABOUT THE AUTHOR

Randy Hartman has a masters degree from the University of Oklahoma. He has spent more than twenty-five years in the people helping profession. Randy has spent a twenty year career with the Army's medical corp.

9 780595 142262